I0138129

COLLECTANEA HERMETICA VOLUME III

A SHORT
ENQUIRY
Concerning the
Hermetick Art.

Addreſs'd to the STUDIOUS
THEREIN.

By a Lover of *Philalethes*.

To which is Annexed,

A Collection from *Kabbala De-nudata*, and Tranſlation of the Chymical-Cabbaliſtical Treatiſe, Intituled, *Æſch-Mezareph*; or, *Purifying Fire*.

LONDON:
Printed in the Year 1714.

Title page for *The Hermetic Art*, Part I, (1714).

COLLECTANEA HERMETICA

EDITED BY

W. WYNN WESTCOTT, M.B., D.P.H.

*(Supreme Magus of the Rosicrucian Society.
Master of the Quatuor Coronati Lodge.)*

VOLUME III.

A SHORT ENQUIRY CONCERNING

THE HERMETIC ART

BY

A LOVER OF PHILALETHES.

1714 & 15.

PREFACE BY
W. WYNN WESTCOTT

AN INTRODUCTION TO ALCHEMY
AND NOTES BY S.S.D.D.

2013
GOLDEN DAWN RESEARCH TRUST

COLLECTANEA HERMETICA
VOLUME III: THE HERMETIC ART

ISBN: 978-1-9269820-3-8.

First published as Volume III of the *Collectanea Hermetica* by Theosophical Publishing Society, 1894.

Revised and Corrected Edition.

20 19 18 17 16 15 14 13   5 4 3 2 1

In the Editorial Content, Notes and Layout Copyright © 2013 by Golden Dawn Research Trust. Introduction © 2013 by Tommy Westlund.

All rights reserved. The Author(s) and Editor have asserted their moral rights to be identified as the Authors of this Work.

No part of this book may be reproduced or utilized in any form or by any means, electronic or mechanical, including photocopying, recording or by any information storage and retrieval system, without permission in writing from the Golden Dawn Research Trust except in the case of brief quotations embodied in critical articles and reviews.

The Golden Dawn Research Trust is NOT affiliated with any Occult Group or Organization. Nor do the Editor and Publisher endorse any Occult Group or Organization.

•••○O○•••

Special thanks to William Morris for his knowledgeable help; to the British Library for a copy of the 1714 edition; and to Ernest Pelletier for copies of Reviews from old occult magazines.

GOLDEN DAWN RESEARCH TRUST
P.O. Box 15964 Austin, Texas 78761-5964 USA

Printed in the United States of America.

Contents

ILLUSTRATIONS

A NOTE

BY THE

EDITOR OF THE SERIES.

THE first volume of the "Collectanea Hermetica" has been well received; indeed the Hermetic Arcanum of Jean d'Espagnet could not fail to interest Alchemic students. There could be no doubt that the second volume of the series, *The Divine Pymander*, of Hermes Trismegistus, would also secure an even greater distribution. In now issuing a reprint of the *Short Enquiry concerning the Hermetic Art*, by A lover of Philalethes, with a Preface by "Non Omnis Moriar," and an "Introduction to Alchemy," by my friend, S.S.D.D., great confidence is felt that this third volume will be equally successful.

W. WYNN WESTCOTT, M.B., D.P.H.

PREFACE

TO THE

"HERMETIC ART."

(PART I.)

THERE is great reason to believe that this *Enquiry into the Hermetic Art*, first published in 1714,[1] led to the composition of the still more extended and more spiritually conceived volume, the *Suggestive Enquiry into the Hermetic Mystery and Alchemy*, which was published anonymously in 1850.[2] This latter volume, which has for many years been unprocurable, and which cannot yet be reprinted by any one unless with the consent of the survivor of the two authors, is an almost complete review of Alchymy on the spiritual plane.

The volume before us has a distinct reference to the science of Alchymy referred to the plane of human improvement, although it is also definitely concerned with the equally possible, though almost incredible power of transmutation upon the material plane.

This Short Enquiry was written with especial reference to the Kabbalistic work, now almost unprocurable, the *Æsch Mezareph*, which is a tractate connecting physical Alchymy with the Kabbalah—so well known *to* refer *to* divine, human and cosmic conceptions; and which system of philosophy has been so very largely used by the late Madame Blavatsky to support and corroborate the wonderful system of human and universal genesis partly unveiled in her great work, *The*

Secret Doctrine of the adepts of the Eastern World. With her wonderful intuition she perceived that the published and still extant Kabbalistic treatises were but debased copies of the more true Chaldee Hebrew doctrine; for she indeed was never entirely initiated into either of the branches of the still extant Kabbalistic and Hermetic secret societies. From the Eastern Light which had dawned upon her so generously, she could indeed criticise, but could never fully comprehend the nature of Kabbalistic illumination.

Dr. Anna Kingsford, the other eminent modern Theosophist or seeker after the true conception of the Divine, although but slightly familiar with the Indian school of thought, was somewhat fully in communion with the doctrines called Hermetic—or by collateral descent,— Rosicrucian.

The anonymous author of this *Short Enquiry* was definitely a Rosicrucian adept, and although his common name has not transpired, yet his identity was known to the initiated occultists of his day and the records of his progress inscribed in the unpublished roll of his branch of the Rosicrucian fraternity.

The *Suggestive Enquiry* chose instead of *Æsch Mezareph*, two other ancient discourses upon Alchymy as the text for its instruction; these were the "Aureus, or Golden Tractate of Hermes," and the "Six Keys of Eudoxus," which formed one of three portions of the famous *Hermetic Triumph*, the other two fragments being named the "War of the Knights," and the "Discourse of Eudoxus and Pyrophilus." The earliest edition, known to me, of these curious tracts, is the French translation of "Limojon de Saint Didier," dated 1699; besides this, there is still procurable the English version of 1723.

It is intended to reproduce these curious essays in succession to the *Æsch Mezareph*, which is already in preparation, and which is certain to interest all true students of the occult sciences, because it points out the analogies between Alchemic tenets and the allegorical explanation of many passages in the Old Testament of the Hebrews.

In order to assist fellow students in their investigations, I have added here a summary of the *Short Enquiry*, and have prevailed upon the learned Soror S.S.D.D., to contribute an "Introduction to Alchemy," which will be found pregnant with meaning by those who have the divine afflatus, although to the ordinary reader, who takes up an Hermetic book only from curiosity, her essay will need to be studied with the closest attention.

A Summary of the *Hermetic Art*.

THE anonymous author commences with a definition of Alchymy, and proceeds to argue that there must be a sound basis for the science because so many authors of different eras and widely separated countries have all agreed upon the essentials of the doctrine and of the art, and that in many instances almost identical results have been described by adepts wholly unknown to each other, although contemporaneous. He very properly urges that the decision of the truth or error of these doctrines can only be rightly judged by other persons who have actually investigated these researches, and the negative evidence of those who have failed, and the judgment of those who have not searched for themselves, is not any criterion by which such intricate forms of philosophy should be estimated. He further insists that the great learning and lives of pious zeal of many of those who gained success in alchymy should demand an *à priori* confidence in the tenets they demonstrated and sought to unfold. Leaving for the time the thread of the argument, he regrets the failures and wasted energies of many who, in defiance of the warnings of true adepts, and in disregard of the conditions which they laid down as essential to success, yet intruded themselves upon this psycho-spiritual path. He points out especially three requirements which were always insisted upon as necessary to attainment of the *Summum Bonum, viz.*, a virtuous life, pure and unsullied by sensual enjoyment from birth to the time of trial, a certain freedom from ordinary social and business liabilities, and the inherent power to comprehend the language of symbol and allegory.

He then warmly supports the alleged necessity for the use by alchymists of symbolism and illustration rather than the plain language of exoteric science; remarking most truly that to the pupil who has in himself the power to succeed, the light of intuitive perception will surely dawn, and that so will he be enabled to appreciate the ideals intended to be conveyed, and at the same time will acknowledge the wisdom of such revealing as is present in the works of the true adepts.

The *Enquiry* then passing superficially to the Assiatic or material plane, yet at all times preserving the actual scheme of spiritual manifestation, considers the grand doctrine of contrast, alluding to the essential differences between Perfect and Imperfect metals, and thus introduces the ideal of the Triune. There are three principles of manifestation and of matter, and even three processes of transmutation. The Universal Solvent or bond of union is then considered, the snowy splendour of Unity standing between the two contrasted forces which form the Dyad. (See the *Sepher Yetzirah.*) This subject is largely commented upon, and allusion is made to the Process even upon the plane of matter, requiring a "Means Mineral" between the two material forms. Many illustrations are then given, notably the doctrines of Sir George Ripley, a Canon of

Bridlington, famous alike as a churchman and as a chemist, who formulated the ideal of the Green Lion as a type of the third element—the Means—by which alone could the extremes be knit in perfect association.

Returning once more to the help of the student, the *Enquiry* recommends that such as mean to succeed should study not only *one* real master in his published works, but several; because each author took care that by one book alone the whole secret could not be learned; and that this was not only to stimulate research and cultivate the intuition, but also lest any unworthy person should obtain so great an acquisition as transmutation, which could be misused as well as turned to good account.

Our author then becomes discursive and suggestive and elucidates (or reveals) the meaning and intention of several symbols and paraphrases, such as the terms "Doves of Diana" and the Caduceus of Hermes, and some of the Kabbalistic allegories such as the story of Naaman, Elisha and Gehazi.

Becoming still more useful to the learner, our author reverts to the requirements and aims of students, telling them plainly that the Great Secret is almost unattainable by study alone, and that a Master is needed, and that a Master will be forthcoming to him or her who has the inherent faculty of culture upon the Alchemic basis; and finally he ends his discourse by encouraging the learner in his efforts by showing the analogies between the seed of gold reproducing gold, and the grain of wheat by which alone is a crop of Wheat to be obtained. The Solar heat of nature in her working to produce a crop for man's needs and benefit, is also a type of the Hidden Fire by which the Alchymist is able to separate the impure from the pure, and to produce the mystic gold from amongst the dross of worldly mind and common matter.

In conclusion, he states, that although the adepts made such free use of allegory, symbol and simile in order to disguise their secret, yet if a man's intuition do but take a firm grasp of one of them, the mystery of a whole series unfolds itself, and the discovery of matters, means and process is achieved, alike on the material plane, and in that higher world where we find Rest in God alone.

N[on] O[mnis] M[oriar]—R.R. et A.C.

[W. Wynn Westcott]

Notes:
1. Parts II and III of *The Hermetic Art* were published a year later in 1715, and they were not reprinted by W. Wynn Westcott.—D.K.
2. *Suggestive Inquiry into the Hermetic Mystery with a Dissertation on the More Celebrated of the Alchemical Philosophers, Being an Attempt Towards the Recovery of the Ancient Experiment of Nature* [by Mary Anne Atwood]. London: Trelawney Saunders, 1850. This book was originally published anonymously, but the Author's name first appeared in the 1918 edition (London: W. Tait).—D.K.

PREFACE

TO THE

"HERMETIC ART."[1]

(PARTS II & III.)

———

THE Readers cannot but perceive for what end they are, in the following Treatise, entertained with the Opinions and Practices of some Men, who labour, or rather toil, in this Enquiry, after that manner, without any Success.

It was done for no other purpose, but to set in our view, in the most strong and lively manner, as well as to explode, such frivolous and foreign Attempts; wherein Men are vainly spending their Time and Money; cheating themselves, and too often others, with Processes and awkward Notions, which are as remote from Truth, Nature, and the Intentions of the Philosophers, as one Pole is from the other.

Such Men are amply described, in a few Words, by *Norton*, *viz*:—

> "They lewdly believe every Conclusion,
> Be it never so false an Illusion:
> If it in Book written they may it find,
> They wean it true; they were so lewd of Mind."[2]

There were such Men in all Ages, as we find by the Philosophers Books. Three Notables Ones (besides many others) *Norton* mentions, *viz*:—

"*Tonsilus*, *Bryan*, and *Halton* in the West,
Ever busy and could practice with the best;
And yet this Science they never found,
For they knew not, the Matters nor the Ground.
But rambled forth, and evermore they sought,
They spent their Life and their Goods to nought,
Among their Receipts which they had wrought."[3]

It is no wonder Men live and die in Error (work or not work) if they neither understand the Matters nor the Ground of this Art. They may boast, with those Three eminent Enquirers, that they can practise with the best, that is upon such foolish Processes, to which Nature is an utter Stranger, how artfully so ever they may be contrived or performed. Nor am I about to deny, but that some them may require more Skill and Cunning in Manual Operation, than the Elixir itself. But as they have no Tendency to it, so they are deservedly of no account in this Art, of whatever Value they may be in others.

As we see the several Artificers in Metals make Wonderful and very Useful Things out of them; but what Affinity have their Works with the Operations of Nature in the Production of them?

So the Skill of the Dyer, in striking the many curious Colours, by his Art, with the Materials afforded by Nature, has no relation to the producing of those Concretes.

Just so it is with those who work-out, with great Ingenuity, various Inventions, by Vulgar Chymical Processes, whereby, it is true, many strange Appearances are produced, and perhaps, for some purposes, useful Preparations, but of no manner of Kin to the secret Art of *Hermes*.

For Secret and Vulgar Chymistry are as different as a Gardener is from a Painter. The latter being altogether busied in his curious Art and manual Skill to make at best but the Appearances or Shadows of things: The other only waits upon and assists Nature in her various Productions of the real things themselves, multiplying the diversity of Species, he handleth, by her Aid and Skill, or in vain are his Attempts.

The Distinction between the Subtleties of Invention, which Art is capable of, and the plain way of Nature's preceding in the Production of Things, seems to have been the whole drift of Sendivogius in his Writings. Whereby, he thought, he should be more serviceable to the Studious, than by perplexing their Studies with Processes, or the crafty Designs of other Philosophers. And pithily tell us what Men were prone to in his time, and the Consequence of it, viz.:— "Men bend their Wits not to things known and familiar, but to such things which not at all, or very hardly, can be done. Wherefore it happens that they are more dextrous in devising curious Subtleties, and such which the Philosophers never thought of, than to attain to the true Processes of Nature, and the right Meaning of Philosophers."[4] So this Art is conversant about the perfecting Metals in Nature's own way; and indeed promoting her farther than she can of herself attain, and when this is done, as is said, in her own way, she is always at hand to assist. Man has nothing to do in each Kingdom, but to remove Impediments, bring Agent and Patient together, and prevent the Accidents, each Kingdom is incident to, and Nature will do the rest. Nature's Way necessarily includes Nature's Pace and Time.

Now, we see, Nature proceeds leisurely, and by imperceptible degrees, in every Generation, even in those which are soonest brought to Perfection; how much more in those which are of longest Duration, as Stones and Metals. How then must it fare with the Precipitate and Hasty, who propose a most expeditious Production of the most perfect of them? When, alas! They are far enough from knowing how to make anyone inferior Gradation; as *Mercury* into *Saturn*, *Saturn* into *Jupiter*, and *Jupiter* into *Luna*: Much less, I say, *Venus* and *Mars*, or any of them, into *Sol*.

These things Philosophers assert not only to be doable, even without the Transmuting Elixir; but to be the very Foundation of the Art of Transmutation: Concerning which, one of them has thus expressed himself, viz.:— "And what does this argue, but that all claim to themselves one Matter, from which all come, and to which all return; and that all things reduced to this Mercurial

Matter, according to the variety of Digestion, may go from one, into another's Species, and alone successively Travel through all? Which Argument, as being true in itself, so also it will remain a firm and inviolable Foundation to this Art."

These things being unknown, in vain does anyone, in this Art, take upon him the Title of a Philosopher. Yea, by the same Art, they can make *Sol* himself stoop to every one of these imperfect States, and travelling through them all, arrive again at his Perfection. Such Operations as these are deservedly called Philosophical and Natural: But O! How far distant are these from the Works of Common Chymists?

Therefore, to conclude, if we are ignorant of the least of these Mutations or Gradations, and cannot set our Foot upon the lowest Step of the Ladder, with what Confidence can anyone boast of being arrived at the top?

Take these things in good part; or, if I have done amiss, forgive and instruct me better.

A LOVER OF PHILALETHA.

Notes:
1. The Preface is reprinted from *The Short Enquiry Concerning the Hermetic Art*, pp. i-x. London, 1715.–D.K.
2. This quote is from "The Ordinall of Alchymie" by Thomas Norton in *Theatrum Chemicum Britannicum*. Edited by Elias Ashmole, 1652.–D.K.
3. "The Ordinall of Alchymie" by Thomas Norton, 1652.–D.K.
4. This was quoted from *A New Light of Alchymie* by Michael Sendivogius. Translated out of the Latin into English by J[ohn] F[rench]. London: Printed by Richard Cotes, for Thomas Williams, 1650.–D.K.

INTRODUCTION[1]

TO THE

"HERMETIC ART."

———

THIS anonymous treatise on the *Hermetic Art* was authored by an alchemist who did not wish for fame, or to portray himself as a teacher. Relying upon certain Masters, the author draws parallels, makes inquiries and elucidates the fundamental processes of the Art, hinting at certain areas where, apparently, many of his fellow alchemists were led astray. His commentaries and illustrative quotes may confuse and discourage readers who seek emblematic images upon which to meditate or a clear ABC book about Alchemy. The treatise, however, contains a multitude of gems for both the alchemist and Golden Dawn Adept.

The author can be viewed as a representative of the Rosicrucian tradition of the late 17th and early 18th centuries. Whereas, Westcott, *et al*, could be viewed as furthering the Rosicrucian current by re-publishing *The Hermetic Art* in the late 19th century. These works demonstrated to the Western world a living esoteric tradition for which Divine providence and the Hermetic societies could provide the Keys.

Westcott published only the first part of the treatise, unfortunately. Nor were the latter two sections captured in Florence Farr's Notes. Significantly, they are now being republished for the first time since 1715. The three parts transform the treatise into a complete and coherent document that will guide the reader in and around the Hermetic labyrinth of Ariadne, where the author's discourses, quotes and the different questioning voices seek to penetrate the veils and allegories of the noblest Art without prostituting it.

It is thus a great honour to write a new introduction to the *Hermetic Art* for the 21ᵗʰ century, continuing in the path of a long historical tradition of Alchemy. This was especially imbued by two of my favourite sources of inspiration in the Golden Dawn tradition, Westcott and Farr, who laid the path a century ago.

Our unknown author also wrote an Preface for Parts II and III, containing a complaint that seems to be timeless concerning not only Alchemy, but any kind of spiritual work: that so many people spend their time and money deceiving both themselves and others in terms of the Art, where elusive theories and experiments lead them further and further away from the foundation of the work.

The treatise is not an attempt to attract more people to study the *Hermetic Art*. Rather, the author seeks to influence the majority of those who are already studying and practicing Alchemy to stop for a moment and ask themselves tough but fundamental questions: Do they know the foundation and basis of the Art? Do they comprehend the theory? Are the pillars of reason and experience built upon solid ground? And most importantly, do they work in accordance with Nature?

We can read the author's criticism of his contemporary alchemists, who prepare various vulgar materials and achieve fascinating effects through chemical experiments, yet which do not belong to the Art of Hermes. We can see a similar situation today, where chemical, psychological and magical artists create evocative art based on alchemical symbolism, but who are still not gardeners working with Nature herself. Or self-proclaimed Adepts and Masters build illusory castles within the *darkness of ignorance* that will only trap consciousness, instead of releasing it or unfolding the divine spark and thereby multiplying the Light.

The notion of Alchemy as a broad or specific term raises several questions. Does it require a general comprehension of a universal Art, which could be worked with in many different ways? Or is it rather a specific operative Art with only one or a very few true substances and techniques available? Is the underlying intention and philosophy able to make more or less anything into Alchemy? Or is such an idea further proof that the secrets of the alchemists have never reached the vulgar world, not even most of those who have studied and practiced it?

When studying the history of the Western esoteric tradition, it is apparent that Alchemy has faded in and out of esteem. The understanding of purpose and means, relation to the religious, philosophical and scientific matrixes, and the way Nature itself is viewed are historically and culturally bound. In particular, if Nature is considered to be fallen, then why should the alchemists study and imitate it to learn its secrets, especially for a pious student of the spiritual? Consider prospect of making gold, producing elixirs of longevity, and reaching the *Summum Bonum*. This has certainly been a stumbling block for many Christians in the past. It also spreads an *archetypical shadow* upon present times, given our tendency to exploit and violate a Nature devoid of any spiritual values.

Scrutinizing the history, philosophy and practice of Alchemy, it becomes apparent how certain axioms reoccur at the foundation of its theory. By utilizing these, we can understand the purpose and extent of Alchemy better.

The alchemist must first study the cycles and processes of Nature to be able to see beyond the surface and comprehend its qualities and characteristics. Thereby, these cycles are imitated, accelerated and refined in the Opus, the aim of which is, in the words of the present treatise, to multiply Light. This practice should further be done with devotion, where prayer and work go hand in hand. The tradition is at once an ancient Art and a progressive Science requiring self-knowledge, perseverance and diligence. There is a correspondence between the outer and the inner, the above and the below. Everything is derived from a primordial matter. Substances can be transformed and transmuted once both the impediments and external and temporary forms break down and are removed. The Agent and the Patient are brought together, where essence is revealed, purified and combined with another principle. Such transmutations occur regularly through birth, life, death and rebirth in both macrocosmic and microcosmic levels. However, like produces like: a lion begets a lion, a flower begets a flower, Man begets its own kind, and gold produces gold. It is therefore of utmost importance to realize the purpose, in order to know with what to work. By means of his or her work, the alchemist therefore becomes a co-creator of Creation's process of refinement, as a true philosopher and lover of wisdom, bringing the hidden powers into action, allowing Life to die in order to be reborn as living and philosophical.

By breaking down the impediments of matter, or the soul's outer shell and alloys—which have been shaped by the ephemeral existence, self, or society—the philosophers lead us into their *Chaos*, where the inner hidden essence or gold can be revealed. This gold is the pure imprint of Divinity within matter, as well as its sacred Fire, which combines the *above* with the *below* in an eternal cycle. From this essence a new form can be created, which reflects and unites both spirit and matter, and heaven and earth, in a divine sanctification of Life and perfection of Light through universal Love. This is the Heavenly Jerusalem, which has no need of the Light of the Sun by Day, nor of the Moon, for there is no Night there.

From this short summary, we can see how the alchemical tradition can in fact be regarded as the foundation of the world's mystery traditions that seek to unveil hidden virtues and qualities, and utilize processes of transformations—

a *philosophia perennis*. On the one hand, it seeks an experience-based knowledge about the relationship between God, Man, and Nature, which microcosmically corresponds with the spirit, soul, and body. Such a knowledge about the matrix of creation and its exoteric and esoteric laws will then allow the alchemist to both pray and work, *ora et labora*, for a lesser and greater transmutation and generation. Experiencing how the inner world corresponds with the outer world and the microcosm with the macrocosm, the alchemist can thus affect both, regardless in which kingdom or realm of consciousness the Opus is carried out.

Alchemy is consequently a study that requires the whole of man. To unveil the abstract symbolism, we need to imprint it in our minds, read, re-read and meditate upon alchemical texts and allegories, and dream about them, contrasting our comprehensions with Nature. Indeed, we need to be possessed by it. Thus it requires self-knowledge, in that we will always express our own ideas and visions through the work.

But even with self-knowledge, and conscious awareness of our projections, a Master is needed to provide the Key that unlocks the Hermetic Art. While we live in a time when a multitude of old and rare alchemical treatises are available, and the Art is once again attracting philosophers and students alike, the need for a Master has not disappeared. So where do we find such a Master? Our author recommends reading and studying several books and taking the philosophers as counsellors, as no single source unveils the Magistery nor explains all its steps. By comparing and analysing how different Alchemists describe the Opus, the persisting student can raise the two mystical pillars of Reason and Experience and open the door to the Mystery.

This exercise only takes us to the gateway between the Mystical Pillars of Hermes. It does not necessarily lead us into the philosophical Light of the Art. A Master or Divine providence is still needed to guide us through the Labyrinth of Ariadne. We may recall how the 3rd century alchemist *Zosimos* of Panopolis explained to his Soror Mystica, *Theosebeia*, that his Master was none other than the Greek natural philosopher *Democritus*, regardless of the fact that more than 600 years separated their worldly life spans. Such a Master can be known through magical imagination, meditation, inspiration and dreams, where we are shown the essence of the operation we are working upon. Or, we can in accordance with the Hermetic tradition, define such a Master as Nature's Light or consciousness. The practical implication and combination of Nature and Divine providence also relates to the first Hermetic Key and its secure lock, as the two legs that will be able to explore the Rosary of the Philosophers.

The traditional Keys to illumination are through the study of the Book of Nature, which will unlock the even more occult Book of Man. With the understanding and the opening of these two Books, a true and philosophical gnosis of God will unfold as the realization and implication of the most Holy and Royal Secret—that secret that all true mystery traditions contain as their root—that which is the end of the beginning. This secret can only be spoken about through allegories, but for a son or daughter of the Art the rays of this Sun will transcend one's perception and transmute and transform Creation.

In alchemical language, this Royal Secret is the Key of the Art that unlocks the first Gate. With the attainment and realization of this Key, every alchemical and spiritual treatise can be discerned, whether it is written from a solar or a lunar perspective. With this Fiery Water, the seeds can be made and brought out from the body. This is the Adept who has unfolded and unveiled solar consciousness and realized the philosophical *Chaos* which contains the Sun, Moon, Stars, and the whole of Heavens and the Earth—a true Body of Light, as our author asserts.

Our author spends the first chapter (Part I); the only one published by Westcott, in describing this most fundamental Key. He talks about the true nature of the Green Lion, the Doves of Diana, the devouring dragon, the Fire of Hermes, the *Menstruum*, and the Fiery Water. If and when this Key is unveiled, the Hermetic gate will be opened and with the help of books and one's own ingenuity, the remaining processes will be clear. This Key is indicated in the famous alchemical saying of "children's play and women's work", which shows a specific process for creating the philosophical salt out of the *Anima Mundi*, marrying above with below. This is also one of two instances where the power is above Nature alone, as the *Alpha* and *Omega*.

The second and third chapters (Parts II and III), however, take the form of a dialogue or debate between our author (now the *Investigator*) and a multitude of alchemical practitioners. They question our author about what still remains obscure. The dialogues are engaged by five representatives (A, B, C, D, & E). Two are active, as they have actually performed the work they describe. Three are passive since they ask questions of work and processes performed by colleagues. In the second chapter, the questions deal with, to the outer eye, profound matters and processes of Alchemy: the problem of destroying the corrosive nature of nitre (*salt-petre*), whether gold should be added to the *Prima Materia* and double mercury, the secret of the *Menstruum* that purify crystals in the cold, the true matter to put into the alchemical furnace, and how to successfully fix Sol and Luna.

The discouraging answer is always the same, as our author, the Investigator, views understandings and operations as vulgar expressions of the Art, created of mistaken symbols for reality and truth for allegories. Nevertheless, he communicates the secret philosophical process, which is also depicted in the *Splendour Solis* emblems.

The third and final chapter articulates more philosophical responses to the questions posed by the five representatives, which eventually explore the duality of Matters as Sol & Luna, Saturn & Rhea, Osiris & Isis, the triune aspect of the Stone and the One and only process.

As all volumes of the *Collectanea Hermetica* were, we can assume, mandatory reading for the Golden Dawn Adepts, it may be fitting to end this introduction with a general outline of the alchemical symbolism of the Golden Dawn.

The Golden Dawn system provides philosophical, spiritual as well as veiled practical keys into the Art of Hermes. In contrast to certain other Hermetic societies, the Golden Dawn does not typically teach specific alchemical keys and techniques in the initiation rituals. It instead presents the candidate with different symbolic experiences clothed in mythical, magical and mystical allegories designed to enhance ones growing awareness of the Hidden Light.

There are great benefits for a student who attempts to unlock the more practical mysteries when aspects of the essence have already been experienced. Personal work is used to extract these mysteries in a continuously circulating process, where the tail of one thing will nurture the head of another thing, until we realize that there is only One breath, inhaling and exhaling, dissolving and coagulating, threefold in essence, quadruple in qualities, pentagonal as Man, hexagonal as Divine, through the seven divine operations.

The alchemical colours related to the three main phases of the Art are one of the first experiences that a student of the Golden Dawn tradition will encounter. These are seen in the cloaks of the three greater Officers of the Outer Order where the Hiereus wears a black cloak; the Hegemon wears a white cloak, while the Hierophant wears red. The peacock's tail of wondrous colours is indicated in the Rainbow of Promise, the Qesheth, which the Zelator will see in the East, and as the

Path of the Chameleon which will guide the various Inner Order work and tools. The initiatic journey throughout the Outer Order will imprint the magico-alchemical processes in one's consciousness. The Adept will then be given the Keys to utilize and unfold further mysteries. The $0°=0°$ formula is the formula of the Magic of Light, whereas the $1°=10°$ formula is the general formula of Alchemy. The Neophyte advances into the black stage of Nigredo, starting to learn techniques of introspection and comprehending esoteric symbolism. True, outer guides are necessary, but the participants wear red socks indicating that the hidden Fire is already present. Indeed, the first thing a Neophyte sees in the Temple is a symbolical expression of that Fire, upon the Banner of the West.

Advancing through the Golden Dawn system, one contemplates diagrams, analyses experiences, learns hierarchies, and practices meditation, whereby the hidden Light of occult Wisdom is gradually unveiled and entered. The position, movement and juxtaposition of Temple Officers and diagrams as well as the various myths behind ritual concepts and God-forms hint at hidden formulas that the Adept will later use. The Adept has not left the darkness, but found the hidden spark in the midst of Mount Abiegnus, the mystical mountain of the Rosicrucians. The Nigredo (blackness) of the Outer Order and the dark Night of Ignorance transforms into the Albedo (whiteness) of the Inner Order, where Diana unveils herself and the Fountain radiates the glorious Morning of Light and Knowledge. The Adept explores the regions of the great Unknown, both within and without, and learns through labour the difference between imagination and fantasia. The Higher Genius and the Divine, through the means of the traditional keys, enable the Adept to transcend into and beyond the elementary and planetary spheres.

Having raised and spiritualised matter, the soul encounters a union with the Mystery that only Silence can express, symbolized by the white alchemical wedding. Thus, the Minor Adept advances to the stage of Major Adept. The white must transmute into the redness of Rubedo. In the work of corporifying the Spirit where the Philosophical Child will be born and nurtured by the rays of Sol & Luna and the double blood of the Lion, there is a return to the earth, to the Dragon on the floor of the Vault. The Exemptus Adept manifests the Philosophical Child into perfection and multiplies the Light of the worlds beyond.

The same is described in the third chapter of this book regarding the riddle of the Sphinx:—

"A Quadrangle or Four Elements are first of all to be considered, from hence we come to the Hemisphere, having two lines, a right and a curve, that is to the White Luna, from thence to the Triangle, which consists of Body, Soul and Spirit, or Sol, Luna and Mercury. The Stone, says Rafis, is a Triangle in its Essence, a Quadrangle in its Qualities. And another adds, a Circle, in its invariable Redness."

From such a general overview of the alchemical process within the Golden Dawn system, there are specific keys hidden therein. Westcott provides a perfect example in a footnote, elucidating the author's description of the relationship between the Burnt Offering, the Doves of Diana, Nogah and Venus. To the Golden Dawn student, this immediately brings to mind the diagram of the Burnt Offering in the 4°=7° Grade of Philosophus, which is placed in juxtaposition with the diagram of the Brazen Sea. These two contain reference to the Fiery Water that does not wet hands, which, from an alchemical perspective, casts forward the Philosophus initiation into the Sephirah of *Netzach*. Later on, it is through the door of Venus that the Adept enters into the mystical Vault of CRC. The sections in this treatise that deals with the Doves of Diana should hence be contemplated in depth by any Golden Dawn Adept.

The Portal initiation continues with the keys for the Magistery of the philosophical Water or the *Menstruum*, drawn from the beams of the Sun and Moon. The energy currents and the sphere in the Temple show the divine nitre and the earthly salt, the heavenly dew and the red Adamic earth. The marriage of these subtle salts and virtues requires a Priest and a wedding bed, and will produce the Agent.

From the initiatic perspective, the Portal process should manifest the *Menstruum* that will dissolve the candidate, congealing or giving birth to the Minor Adept. This is accomplished through the marriage of opposites, symbolized by the Cross, bringing forward the analogy of the human with its corruptible body and its relation with the ocean of consciousness. From a magical and hermetic perspective, we need to fully unveil the Doves of Diana so that the poison of the Dragon will be transmuted into the most precious elixir. This is the task of the Adept who seeks to become more than human, unfolding the mystical Rose that blooms upon the Cross of Victory.

Contrary to materialistic beliefs, the Great Work is not essentially focused upon the manufacture of gold. Rather, it is the Art of understanding the origin of worlds in order to create on a microcosmic scale. In a word, it is to be the confidant of the Source. The Great Work is especially the crowning of knowledge and understanding. Thus, the Wise knows the past and future of the worlds and understands its mysteries. Applying this spiritual concept on a physical level may then accomplish the transmutation of plants, minerals, metals, and the bodies of consciousness; the purification of our "I" energy going hand in hand with the process of the Great Work.

Such are the philosophical gems of the Hermetic tradition that run as the Scarlet Thread of Ariadne throughout all volumes of the *Collectanea Hermetica*, where the secret philosophy is expounded for those seeking the Divine and Mysterious Truth.

"Thus have the Philosophers pointed out this Secret Art under Veils and Allegories, not to prostitute it, no; God and Nature forbidding; it is a Science too excellent and admits of no compare, though there are many very useful ones, but this may rather be said, virtually, to contain them all, and is even the best Expositor of Divinity itself, not only by showing the Creation and Destruction of the World, but the true Figure of Mortification, Regeneration, Redemption and Exaltation, set before the Eyes of the Body, and which are in a most lively manner impressed upon the Soul; and the Mind is so furnished with the Knowledge of a Trinity in Unity, as not to admit of a doubt concerning so Divine and Mysterious a Truth."

– A Lover of Philaletha.

TOMMY WESTLUND,
Stockholm, Sweden,
July 2013.

AN INTRODUCTION
TO ALCHEMY.

—⋗∶⋖—

WRITERS on Alchemy are in the habit of making so many prefatory remarks on their own account, that their books stand in very little need of preface; unless indeed, the Editor undertakes to reveal the secrets which the Author is so careful to conceal. I must at once say I am not prepared to do this, but to one thing, I can with advantage call your attention, which is that the study of Alchemy, above all other branches of Occult Science, demonstrates the value of Analogy in our search after the real meaning of the mysteries of man and his relation to the Universe. The process of transmutation, which displays a series of colours, recalls the Religion of the Egyptians, symbolising as it did, the blackness of night, the rainbow colours of dawn, the whiteness of noon, and the red glow of evening. The first stage of this symbolism alludes to the blackness of ignorance, the chaotic darkness of men who reject the keys to the secret of the Universe, which are to be found in the rainbow colours; to the vibrations of sound, to scents, tastes, feelings, and subtle psychical impressions. When a man's mind begins to grasp the order and relation of such sense impressions as these, he bids fair to pass from the darkness of ignorance to the white light of wisdom, and perhaps eventually to attain to the imperial purple which clothes the elect.

To do this he must, within himself, possess the divine gift of *wonder*; for it is through this faculty that he raises himself above the cares of life. The man, whose curiosity carries him from the contemplation of the manifestation to the contemplation of its causes, is the man whose instincts are preparing him to undertake the Great Work.

Content is fatal; the man who is content with anything, who does not feel in his most successful moments, during the most sacred earthly joys, a keen sense of want and disappointment, can never hope to find the Stone of the Wise—True Wisdom and Perfect Happiness.

The happy are sufficiently rare, however, for me to hope that few of my readers will be deterred from the study of Alchemy by what I have said. We have all been taught to look with horror upon Medusa's head, with the serpents twisting round its face, the terror of which turned all to stone who gazed upon it. But we must, if we would learn the secret wisdom of the ages, learn to long for a glance from those wonderful eyes, which will bestow upon us the gift of indifference to personal joys and sorrows. For the wise man must be as a precious stone; a centre of light to all that approach him; giving joy to others, because he contains the image of the highest joy in himself; desiring nothing from the world, drawing his inspiration from the supernal light—that "Wisdom Goddess" who wears the serpent crowned head upon her shield.

Well has Robert Fludd said:— "Be ye changed from dead stones into living philosophical stones. Be equal with God. Ye hear all these things but ye believe not. Oh miserable mortals, who do so anxiously, run after your own ruin."

Then the philosopher points out the futility of the ordinary man of petty aims and weak will, never gaining the goal of the higher, or for the matter of that, the lower Alchemy.

"Oh thou miserable one, wilt thou be more happy?
Oh thou proud one, wilt thou be elevated above the
circles of this world?
Oh thou ambitious one, wilt thou command in
Heaven above this earth, and thy dark body?
Oh ye unworthy, will ye perform all miracles?
Know ye rejected ones, of what nature it is, before
ye seek it."

So it comes to the old, old teaching, Gnothi Seauton, Know thyself; until by deep thought and meditation, words have become more than words to thee; until thou hast analysed them, separated them, transposed them into every conceivable form, and finally extracted from them, their quintessence and spiritual meaning, thou wilt understand no word that the ancient philosophers speak to thee.

Take now the loose meaning attached to such a word as imagination; in these materialistic days it has become synonymous with extravagant fancy, if not with lying: but hear what Paracelsus says of imagination as an occult manifestation of power:— "Man has a visible and invisible workshop. The visible one is his body, the invisible one his imagination. . . . The imagination is a sun in the soul of man acting in its own sphere, as the sun in our system acts on the earth. Wherever the latter shines, germs planted in the soil grow, and vegetation springs up; the imagination acts in a similar manner m the soul, and calls forms of life into existence. ... The Spirit is the master, imagination the tool; and the body the plastic material. Imagination is the power by which the will forms sidereal entities out of thoughts, it can produce and cure disease."

Perhaps this passage will give new light to those who have lately treated this faculty with such contempt, in dealing with the subject of hypnotism.

In truth, Imagination is the power of forming images in our minds. It is the development and intensification of an idea, which first exists, is then conceived passively in the thought sphere; then the mind (perceiving the idea can be used) brings desire into play, which is developed into an act of Will, and this converts the passive conception of the idea into an active Imagination. So begins the magical process, the rest it is not for me to divulge.

I will only add on this subject the saying of Eliphaz Levi, that:– "The first matter of the Magnum Opus is both within and about us, and the intelligent will, which assimilates light, directs the operations of substantial form, and only employs chemistry as a very secondary instrument."

The *Suggestive Enquiry into the Hermetic Mystery and Alchemy*, published a century later than the work under our consideration, points out the method which should be employed in the exhaustive analysis of the nature of man, so necessary to the completion of the great work. He says:– "Metempsychosis takes the human identity (or consciousness) from animal existence to the ethereal elements of its original formation."

That is, in thinking inwardly with calm and philosophic mind we can pass from the manifested life we see and feel, to the motive power of that life; and finally to the cause of the motive power; from the mundane to the supra-mundane; from the intellectual to the intelligible; from the earth to the firmament; from water to the fiery rays of heat emerging from the central light which is the source of all things.

The same book continues:– "These elements are the universal fundamentals of nature: only in the Human form can they attain that supremacy of reason which returns to its first cause."

Reason is the light which guides us. Let me hasten to add how necessary it is to distinguish between the false reason, and the Heavenly Reason which we perceive when intuition is purified; and we rise above the lower passions. The false reason is merely an image set up by our unbalanced forces to justify us in evil doing. Well has it been said, that when we find ourselves seeking to justify ourselves by giving reasons for our actions, we have been doing something we are secretly ashamed of.

True Reason is the clear light descending upon us from that which is above all pretence. It was a communion with this faculty, that Saint Thomas à Kermpis desired when he told those who would detain him, he must leave them, as one was waiting for him in his cell. False reason seeks to justify itself with much argument; Pure Reason knows Truth, and can afford to be silent.

So continues the *Suggestive Enquiry*:— "In the Human form only is it possible to comprehend the Divine form; when it has done so by a triplicate growth of Light in the understanding consciously allied, it emanates a fourth form, truthful, godlike, being the express image of its person magically portrayed."

I think I have said enough to show that the Alchemist undertakes no light task. I can hold out no hope of success to those who still retain an absorbing interest in the world. *In* the world Adepts may be, but not *of* it. Alchemy is a jealous mistress, she demands from pupils no less than life; for her sake you must perform the twelve labours of Hercules; for her you must descend into Hell, for her sake you must ascend into Heaven. You must have strength and patience, nothing must terrify you, the joys of Nirvâna must not tempt you; having chosen your work, you must to this end purify yourself from perishable desires, and bring down the light of the shining ones, that it may radiate upon you here on earth. This is the work of the Alchemist; his true ideal is also the highest ideal of Eastern Theosophy; to choose a life that shall bring him in touch with the sorrows of his race rather than accept the Nirvâna open to him; and like other Saviours of the world, to remain manifested as a living link between the supernal and terrestrial natures.

S[APIENTIA] S[APIENTI] D[ONO] D[ATA]—R.R. *et* A.C.

[Florence Farr]

THEATRUM CHEMICUM
BRITANNICUM.

CONTAINING

Severall Poeticall Pieces of our Famous
English Philosophers, who have written
the *Hermetique Mysteries* in their owne
Ancient Language.

Faithfully Collected into one Volume,
with Annotations thereon,

By ELIAS ASHMOLE, *Esq.*

Qui est Mercuriophilus Anglicus.

THE FIRST PART.

Serpens et Bufo gradiens sup terra, Aquila volans, est nostru Magisteriu.

LONDON,
Printed by *J. Grismond* for NATH: BROOKE, at the
Angel in *Cornhill*. MDCLII.

Title page for *Theatrum Chemicum Britannicum*, (1652).
One of the Key books for Quotations in *The Hermetic Art*.

A SHORT
ENQUIRY

Concerning the

Hermetick Art.

Address'd to the STUDIOUS

THEREIN.

By a Lover of *Philalethes.*

To which is Annexed,

A Collection from *Kabbala De-nudata*, and Translation of the Chymical-Cabbalistical Treatise, Intituled, *Æsch-Mezareph*; or, *Purifying Fire.*

LONDON:
Printed in the Year 1714.

The Hermetic Art, Part I was first published in 1894 by Theosophical Publishing Society, London as part of the *Collectanea Hermetica* series.

This edition was published by The Golden Dawn Research Trust in 2013.

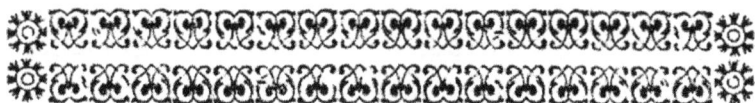

THE HERMETIC[1] ART.[2]

PART I.

THIS Art, of bringing all Imperfect Metals to Perfection, hath been asserted for Truth, by Men of almost every Degree, in most Ages of the World; many of whose Books are extant.

2. They have declared, that they have made and possessed this great Treasure, which not only brings all Imperfect Metals to the Perfection of *Sol* and *Luna*[3] (according to the Quality of the Medicine), but healeth all manner of Diseases in Human Bodies, even renewing Youth and prolonging Life.

3. Those Authors, from Age to Age, have justified one another's Testimony;[4] alledging, as a farther Proof of the Art, that all that have understood it, have written most agreeingly of it, though contemporary, and unknown to one another in Person, or by Writing.

4. How far these Men's Writings have obtained, a very little Enquiry may serve; for most Men look upon these (Alchemic) Books only as Cunningly-devised Fables, and the Art itself as altogether impossible.[5]

5. To which the (Alchemic) Authors answer, That it is not Lawful, nor Commendable to reprobate an Art, by Judges who are ignorant of its Laws as well as the Facts; and that the Ignorant Negative of such, is by no means sufficient to set aside the Affirmative Knowledge of so many Men of Unquestionable

Credit, Piety, and Virtue,—supported by Arguments and Circumstances of Uncontestable Force.

6. From which, together with the Excellency of the Things themselves *(viz.,* Long Life and Riches, *vide* the *Way to Bliss),*[6] many have been induced to believe and seek after this Art.

7. It is the Melancholy View that I have taken of these Men, that have occasioned the putting my own Thoughts into the Order you find them, hoping no Master will be offended, nor any Enquirer displeased.

8. When I compare, I say, the variety of these Men's Fortunes, Capacities and other Qualifications, with those the *Philosophers* have laid down for Men like to succeed, it fills me with Pity, and makes me almost tremble to rehearse the words of Norton,[7] *viz.:—*

> "That of a Million, hardly Three,
> Were e'er ordain'd for Alchymy."

9. O sad Tidings to such Men! Whose impaired Healths, injured Fortunes and barren Practice, renders them more unfit every day than other, and instead of attaining that which should crown their Labours with success, are at length in danger of *denying,* if not *cursing* the Art itself.

10. I would pretty thoroughly enquire from whence this ill success, which attends the generality of Enquirers, proceeds, and accordingly shall mention a few chief Impediments,[8] in my Opinion.

11. *First;* But few of those that seek this Art, are qualified, according to the *Philosophers,* for attaining it; for they assert, "That to find it requires the whole Man;[9] as well as that, when found, it possesses him: Also that it is never found of any by Chance, or by accidental Trials, and casual Experiments;" and that unless the Mind[10] be kindled with a Beam of Divine Light, it will not be able to penetrate this most hidden Science.

12. These with many more Cautions, are plentifully set down in their Books, on purpose to *inform* and *reform* a great

many Persons too rashly concerned in these things; and yet how few take their Advice! Undertaking this Study with much less than half the Man; constantly trying Experiments that have *no Authority* but their own *idle Fancy*; and consequently have Minds, in respect to this Science, as dark as Midnight.

13. Then add to these an almost Insuperable Difficulty, (hard enough to be overcome by those that can spare even the whole Man and are very cautious in their Practice, as having a pretty good Understanding of Natural Things in general, and of the Mineral Kingdom in particular); and that is *the Subtlety of Stile* so peculiar to *Hermetic Philosophers*.

14. Of this they often warn us, telling us also, that if it were not for this, they could not disclose, and at the same time hide their Secret. And though this be a Paradox, *that at the same time they give light, they darken*, yet they affirm it for Truth, with many other things hard enough to be understood; which yet must be understood before anyone can profit by them, witness Geber,[11] Sendivo,[12] &c.

15. Also Norton has given a hint of this mysterious way of Writing,[13] and which indeed sufficiently shows that it will obscure, whether we can discern its Instruction or not, *viz*.:—

> "If you consider how the Parts of Works
> Be out of Order set by the Old Clerks."

16. This breaking to pieces of the several Works, makes it almost impossible for a Tyro to make their Writings *Tally*; any one part not being rightly applied, the whole is incomplete.

17. Another tells us he has done this, by *mixing Unusual Candour with Philosophical Subtleties*, in such a manner as would render their Secret safe, though openly told; Nor is he wanting to admonish his *Reader* to be cautious in these things, *viz*.:—

> "—Yet beware,
> That thou mistake not; for I do aver,
> A mingled Doctrine these Lines do declare;

For both ways in this Book of mine do claim a share:
Learn to distinguish every Sentence well,
And know to what Work it doth appertain.
This is great Skill, which few, as I can tell,
By all their Reading, yet could e'er attain;
And yet of Theory, this is the main."

18. Wherefore it is obvious, there is no possibility of success, 'till it be learned to which Work their Sayings relate; which indeed is not easy, and is the top of Theory; nor can any speed upon any other, though never so finely spun, or fondly embraced.

19. And though *Philosophers* do sometimes affirm their Matters to be many, and their Works also; yet they very often, with equal Authority and Truth, assert the contrary; Artephius[14] saith:—

"Tho' we say in many places, *take this,* and *take that;* yet we mean, that it behoveth thee to take ONE THING.[15] For these things are so set down by the envious Philosophers to deceive the Unwary. ... Do'st thou, Fool, believe, that we do openly teach the Secret of Secrets? And do'st thou take our Words according to the literal Sound? Know assuredly, he that takes the Words of other Philosophers according to the ordinary Signification and Sound of them, he doth already wander in the midst of the Labyrinth, having lost *Ariadne's* Thread,[16] and hath as good as appointed his Money to Perdition."

20. By means of these seeming Contradictions, bolder steps have been taken by some of them in discovering this Art, than otherwise they would have done, and even some have dared to imitate, nay, so much as to repeat.

21. From hence I infer, That as much has been communicated to the World as can be expected, or that God will yet suffer to be discovered by Writing. For this Art is declared, by those that have knowingly written of it, to be under his immediate

Protection. Likewise that those that come to the Knowledge of it, shall admiringly wonder at its Preservation; and that which will augment their wonder, will be, that so slender a Vail secures it; and which God makes a sufficient Guard against all the Attacks made by the unworthy: *Vide Sendivo, etc.*

22. Likewise, that as soon as any one discerns[17] the Intention of the Philosophers, from the seeming Sense of the Letter, the dark *Night* of Ignorance will fly away, and a glorious *Morning* of Light and Knowledge will break forth: When *Diana*[18] will unveil herself, Bathing in that most pleasant *Fountain* so much sought.

23. And that he will find himself in the High Road of Nature which is that *Secret Way* of Philosophers,[19] *viz.,* most *easy, delightful* and *speedy;* in which are no Storms, no Heterogeneities, nor any Fire, but the gentle one of Generation.

24. Norton asserts, That there are but few Clerks that comprehend this Work, it being truly Philosophical. And he saith, That in this Work you must not begin with Quicksilver[20] and Metals, as if in another Work you might; which other Work, *he adds,* if it be done in three Years, would be a blessed Chance, and which belongs to great Men; advising poor Men not to meddle with it, for that Errors in it may be committed above a Hundred ways; that it is a Work of Pain and Labour, as well as full of Perils.

25. That these things are so, we are sorrowfully confirmed, by a Modern Author, as is so well known by many, in his *Introitus Apertus ad Occlusum Regis Palatium.*[21]

26. Now as their Works differ, so their Waters[22] or Mercuries differ also; for if you would calcine a perfect Metal, it must be done with Mercury; but if you would dissolve an imperfect Body *(which is in the way to Perfection)* it must be done with *Mercurial Water,* which is the *Dew* or *Rain Water* of Philosophers.

27. The perfect Body[23] is calcined with a gross Humidity, and by a tedious Labour; but the imperfect Body is dissolved

and purified in a much more subtle Mercury, by an easy Fire and little Toil.

28. And though this subtle *Menstruum* be the Mercury of the imperfect Body, yet it will (for a certain purpose) dissolve *Sol*, as warm Water dissolves Ice, and will make its Body a mere Spirit.

29. This is the Fountain[24] of Chymical or Hermetic Philosophy, concerning which it is said:—

"He that exactly knows the Magistery of this Water, no Words, or Secrets of Philosophers, Sayings, Writings or Enigmas, will be concealed from him. And further, that it is stupendous in its Virtues, and the things out of which it is immediately drawn, are most secret above all others; also the means of extracting it most wonderful. In the Knowledge of which, all their Fires, Weights and Regimens lie hid."

30. The same Author affirms, that none can imagine its *Splendour*, except they see it, and then you will think you look upon a certain Celestial Body. Believe me, *saith he*, I have seen this *Snowy Splendour*.[25]

31. *Sendivo* not only confirms the same in Words to this effect, *viz.*, Believe me, for I beheld it, that that Water was as white as Snow, but adds, from whence it was drawn, *viz.*, From the Beams of the *Sun* and *Moon*.[26]

32. Nor is this said by him only, but by many more; I shall instance a few.

33. Artephius asserts, "That it is drawn from the Beams of the Sun and Moon, yea, that this dissolving Water is the Soul of the Sun and Moon, their moist Fire, and the only Agent in the World for this Art."

34. The Author of *Hermetic Arcanum*,[27] saith, "Let thy Mercury draw its Original from both these Lights."

35. Flamel, speaking of the Sun and Moon, saith, "They are of a Mercurial Source, and Sulphurous Original."

36. Another, *viz.,* the Author of the *Way to Bliss,* saith:—
"That as the Sun is the Father of all things, and the Moon
his Wife the Mother, (for he sends not down these begetting
Beams immediately, but through the Belly of the Moon) and
this double Spirit is carried in a Wind and Spirit into the Earth,[28]
to be made up and nourished."

37. Which double Spirit or Flame, *Geber* calls the *immediate Matter of Metals.*

38. You very well know, that *Hermes* himself, as well as most
of his Followers, agree in these things; and it is our Business to
observe wherein they do agree. *Arnold* says,[29] "In our Imperfect
Metal, there are the Sun, and Moon in Virtue and near Power."
The Philosophic Work begins with this Heavenly Mercury, and
an imperfect Body purified.

39. "There is a pure Matter" (saith another) "which is
the Matter of Gold, containing in itself the Heat that giveth
Increase." *(Fire of Generation.)* This is locked under thick Folds
in common Gold; nor is it to be extracted, but by a strong and
tedious Decoction, which is a Work liable to many Errors, and
hath always occasioned those that wrought in it to complain of
the length and trouble of it. But in the other Work, the Body
is soon dissolved, by a sweet and kindly Bath, or moist Fire.[30]

40. As the former Path requires much Pains and Patience
to effect the Work, so this requires great Skill and Application
to find it out, it being deeply concealed. The Masters of these
Secrets do also affirm, that these Works (which are all one in
the {End, but nor in the}[31] Beginning) may be conjoined, and
made their grand Medicine. And I have been informed, that
the way of making them one is but slenderly hid. For should
they but change some Words (which they affect to use in order
to conceal it) of one[32] Syllable, and sometimes of two, for
others of three, and sometimes of four or more, it would not
be difficult, for a Tyro, to conceive it. And the Reason given
for this slender Covering is, that if anyone should discern it,

and yet be ignorant of the Means of both it would be of little avail; and that if he knew the Means, he could not long remain ignorant of the Practice. So that the Knowledge of the Means seems absolutely necessary in the first place.

41. These Norton calls his "Means Mineral," which, he saith, "are no other than Magnetia[33] and Litharge[34] her Brother." And he asserts that "to clarify them is the foulest Work of all."

42. And though he makes these Means two, yet he tells you how they differ, *viz.*, as a *Mother* from her *Child*, or as a *Male* from a *Female*: Which we see brings his to the general Doctrine of Philosophers, *viz.*, *Agent* and *Patient*, which seems to be their *one* Intention, whatever Skill they use to perplex their Sayings.

43. Litharge, he says, is "a subtle Earth, brown, ruddy, and not bright."

> "Old Fathers call'd it a thing of vile Price,
> For it is nought Worth by way of Merchandise;
> No Man that findeth it would bear it away,
> No more than they would an Ounce of Clay."[35]

44. He likewise saith, it is "not to be sold in all Christian Ground, but thou must be fain to make it."

45. *Magnetia* is fair and bright, known by few, and is found *in High* Places as well as *in Low* and called by Plato, *Titanos;* these are the Materials to make *Elixir;* and addeth:—

> "This Secret never was before this Day
> So truly showed, take it for your Prey."

46. Now to apply these things to the Doctrine of Philosophers; Litharge must be their *Brass*, or Philosophical Sol; *Magnetia* must be understood to be their *Subtle Humidity*, or Philosophical Mercury; which is *Living* and not only so, but *Enlivening; Clean* and not only so, but *Cleansing; Volatile*, and not only so, but *Volatilizing*, even the most fixed Body of *Sol;* and is the Radical Moisture of Metals.

47. How this is attained, is worthy our Enquiry, and whether they agree in the manner of preparing it, as well as from whence it is to be drawn, *viz.,* From the *Sun* and *Moon*; for it seems it must have the Influences of both.

48. But to collect these Virtues requires a *Mean*, as Ripley[36] hath it, speaking of the Green Lion:—[37]

"He is the mean, the Sun and Moon between, *&c.*"

49. Also the Author of *Hunting the Green Lion*[38] saith:—

"The Lion is the Priest, the Sun and Moon the Wed;
Yet they were both born in the Priest's Bed."

50. By which *Green Lion* another saith:— "All Philosophers understand Green Gold, multipliable, spermatic, and not yet perfected by Nature; Or *Assa Fœtida*, because in the very first of this Operation or Distillation, a white Fume with a stinking Smell exhales." It was by this strong scent that *Flamel* knew this Subject.

51. That this agrees with the rest of the Philosophers, I need not enlarge to show, it being well known to them who read their Books.

52. This Distillation, *Hermes,* as well as many others, declares must be made by a gentle Fire, by little and little, with great Discretion, lest the *thick* be mixed with the *thin*, the *subtle* with the *gross*, or the *foul* with that which is *clean*. Lully[39] is very famous for his witty Description of this Operation, under the Figure of *Distilling of Wine*, which he sometimes also calls *Juice of Lunaria*, from which he extracts the Sweat with *a gentle Fire*, in the form of *a white Water.*

53. This is also called by other Names, as *Adrop, Saturn,*[40] *Brass, Leprous Gold*, and *Imperfect Body*; and which they all agree lies in great Obscurity, *saturnine* and *foul*, in the making of which there is a *great Stink*; that it is *not fixed*, a *Medium* between a *Metal*, and a *Mineral* partaking of the Nature of both, and *very crude*, containing an *Argent Vive*, which is the Basis and

Ground-work of their precious Medicine. And thus, saith the Philosopher, "you will come to understand how Saturn contains the greatest Secret in this Art." This is the "Golden Branch, so much concealed, which all the Groves with Shadows overcast, and gloomy Valleys hide, and which will follow none, but him that knows Dame *Venus's* Birds and him to whom of Doves a lucky Pair," &c.—*Hermetic Arcanum*.[41]

54. The Masters of this Science agree with *one Voice* in this, *viz.*, "That this Matter must be exactly purified, and dissolved into an Argent Vive, of such Virtues as are nowhere else possible to be found."

55. This is performed by a wonderful *Cohobation*; the Number of which Cohobations are much varied: But in this they all agree, that there must be so many, till a *total Dissolution* and *perfect Purity* be known.

56. The time of doing this, some will have it, is hinted in *Hermetic Arcanum* where it is said, "Make the Dragon to drink Thrice the Magical Number Seven, until having drunk, he put off his hideous Garments."[42]

57. Thus, I say, Three times Seven is Twenty-One, which some will interpret Days, and to which some other Philosophers seem to agree; but whether these are One and Twenty Days or Cohobations, he will rightly determine, who shall be blessed with the Knowledge of their "Light bringing Venus, and Horned Diana."—*Hermetic Arcanum*.

58. Likewise the Philosophers agree in the Virtues of this Water, *viz.*, that as it partakes of the Natures of *both Sexes*, so it acts the part of both, *viz.*, *Dissolving* and *Congealing*. For they assert, "That it will Congeal itself into a Lunar or a Solar Nature, (according to the design of the Workman) without any addition whatsoever."

59. There are also some Cautions given concerning Proportion in *Compounding* the *Imperfect Body*, as well as with relation to its *Dissolution*; for that in case of *undue Weight* or

Measure, the Virtue will be much diminished, if not altogether spoiled. But if a *due Proportion* be observed, and a *proper Fire* given, the *true Sign* will follow.

60. The true Union between the *imperfect Leprous Body*, and its Water, they have deeply concealed, as the Philosophers own, and Searchers find; because as they say, "the rest is so easy in the Work of Generation, that it is hardly to be missed, by one that hath attained their wonderful Mercury, so united and purified."

61. Concerning which, they have declared, they have given such hints as are sufficient to an enlightened Mind; and that none shall ever dare to do it more openly, without a Curse from God.

62. But all have not done it with the same Candour, nor by the same *Similes* and *Enigmas*; *The New Light*[43] under that of Chalibs; the *Way to Bliss*, by that of the *Witty Fire of Hermes*, and so of the rest, Norton says:—

> Bacon[44] did it darkly, in his Three Letters all;
> But Raymond[45] better, in his Art general."

63. And since the Readers can expect no better Account from me, concerning the *Means* and *Medium* of this Wonderful *Union*, than the Philosophers have learnt in their Books,[46] I must refer them for more ample Satisfaction and Information therein. For, as Norton saith:—

> "Trust not therefore to Reading of one Book,
> But in many Authors' Works ye may look.
> *Liber librum aperit*, saith Arnold the great Clerk;
> Anaxagoras[47] said the same for his Work,
> Who that slothful is in many Books to see,
> Such one in Practice, prompt shall never be."

64. The Reason he gives for thus Reading and Comparing many Books, is, that:—

> "Every each of them taught but one point, or twain,
> Whereby his Fellows were made certain,

How that he was to them a Brother,
For every of them understood each other."

65. I have mentioned Norton the more, because it appears to me, that he and his Contemporary Ripley, have written very Learnedly of this Art, and wonderful Agreeingly, through both writ near the same time, and very probably one in *England* and the other *abroad*; and for ought I can meet with, were not known to one another at that time. Nor can one suppose that Norton had seen Ripley's *Compound of Alchymie,* since it was written but six years before his *Ordinall.* Books, *of that kind especially*, did not in those days come abroad quickly: Nor doth Norton, when he reckons up some that had written excellently of *Proportion*, take any notice of Ripley, who beyond all questions hath in that excelled.

66. This Harmony in Authors, that have written of the Art at the same time, and unknown one to another, a Modern Adept of the same Nation with the two before mentioned, has brought as a convincing Argument (among others) to prove its Being; and which, with me, has great Weight, and seems to serve his purpose.

67. This Author has professed to have outdone all that went before him, discovering such things, he says, *as the World was barren enough of before*, yet his Disciples have much complained of their ill success; notwithstanding they have seemed to understand him more fully than the *other Philosophers*, insomuch that many have concluded *his way* of proceeding in this Art to be *different* from many of theirs. Nay, at length some have so ill rewarded his Candour, as to charge him with being ignorant {himself} of those things he so solemnly professeth to be true, and of which his Accusers are unworthy.

68. It seems he foresaw his Readers would thus misconstrue his Writings, and therefore he *here* and *there* scatters some *necessary Cautions* for those that would receive them.

69. "Nor let any expect," saith he, "Comfortable Doctrine in our Books, who know not the true Keys, by which our Matter is brought forth from Darkness into the Light: For verily though we write for the Enlightening a true Son of Art, yet also for the fatal Blinding of all such Owls and Bats, who cannot behold the Light of the Sun, nor can endure the Splendour of our Moon. To such we propound rare Tricks, suiting to their sordid Fancy: To the Covetous, an easy way without Expense: To the Hasty, Rash and Unstable, multiplicity of Distillations." {Again,}

70. "In the World our Writings shall prove like a curious edged Knife;[48] to some they shall carve out Dainties, to others they shall serve only to cut their Fingers. It is the Sign of an Owl,[49] to be blinder, by how much the Sun shines brighter.—If thou wilt be heedless, thou may'st sooner stumble at our Books, than at any thou didst ever read in thy Life. ... Take this from one that knows best the Sense of what he has written; where we speak most plainly, there be most circumspect, (for we do not go about to betray the Secrets of Nature) especially in those places which seem to give Receipts so plain as you would desire, suspect either a Metaphor, or else be sure that something is suppressed which thou wilt hardly find (without Inspiration) of thyself; yet to a Son of Art, we have written that which never heretofore was by any revealed."

71. I might add many more Cautions of other Authors, as well as of this, concerning the *Difficulties which attend the Reading of their Books*; and had not mentioned what I have, but that it appeared the more necessary to mention some of this Author's, because almost every Body has taken up an Opinion, that he is more easily understood than the rest; but how profitably, themselves may judge.

72. We should not be just to ourselves, if we should be ignorant that when any of them have made a Discovery *of this*

or *the other Part of the Work*, they have not Balanced it with such Obscurities which are not easily discerned; especially *by the Unwary*.

73. And therefore if the Students in this Art, and particularly of *this Author's Works*, did believe the Philosophers had *Cunning* equal to their *Skill* and would but take the Advice given by them, they would not have room to Censure the *Philosophers* but themselves.

74. For what could anyone have said, more to have deterred Enquirers from rash Conclusions, either in Theory or Practice, than this Author has done? *viz.:—* "Venture not," saith he, "to practice barely upon my Words: For know that what I have only hinted, is far more than what I have discovered; and what I have declared to thy first Apprehension, most openly, hath yet its lurking Serpent under the green grass;[50] I mean some hidden thing, which thou oughtest to understand; which thou, being Cocksure at first Blush, wilt neglect."

75. The fond Notion which Men have entertained, of understanding this Author's Writing more perfectly or easier than the rest of the Masters is to me an Argument of his great skill in that peculiar way of Writing, which the *Hermetic Philosophers* profess and value themselves upon, *viz.*, to be able *openly to show the Art to the Sons of it*, and yet *secure it from the Unworthy*.

76. That this is true, all their Writings show; for some of them have learned the *Art from Books* as they own; which could not be, if it were not taught in them. These indeed are very few in comparison to those that Learn it not, though they read the same Books, but not the same things in them. As this Author hath again excellently described such Men, *viz.:—* "Some, I know, will serve my Book, as they have served others; out of it they will read their own Phantastic Processes, which I never dreamt of, nor yet are they in Nature.—Though we write in *English*, yet our Matter will be as hard as *Greek* to some, who

will think they understand us well, when they misconstrue our Meaning most perversely. Nor is it imaginable, that they, who are Fools in Nature, should be Wise in our Books, which are Testimonies to Nature."

77. As this Author hath professed an extraordinary esteem[51] for Ripley, and (in many things) has imitated *his Candour*, yet he has so manifestly compounded it with the *Craft of Norton*, that it is hard to distinguish them, and which well deserves the Cautions he hath given, and his Readers' Care therein.

78. He has in his Books led us some part of the way under such *Philosophical Veils*, as have been pretty easily seen through by most that read them with Application; who no sooner discover some of his *Metaphors*, but overcome with Joy, and exalted with an Opinion of their own Abilities, presently cry out, *we have found! We have found!* And what have they found? Why their way into a *Labyrinth*.[52]

79. For at the end of this short Walk, he hath set up one *Metaphor*, harder to be understood than all the rest, *viz.*, The *Doves of Diana*. This stands at the Entrance into a great *Labyrinth*, in which are abundance of Enquirers rambling at this day; many of them undiscerned by one another.

80. I have taken several Turns in it myself, wherein one shall meet with very few; for it is so large, and almost every one taking a *different Path*, that they seldom meet.

81. But finding it a very *Melancholy Place*, I resolved to get out of it, and rather content myself to walk in the *little Garden before the Entrance*, wherein *many things*, though not *all*, were orderly to be seen. Choosing rather to stay there, and contemplate on the *Metaphor set up*, than venture again into the *Wilderness*; in which I heard the *Noise and Voices* of several *strange and devouring Creatures*, (some of which I had with difficulty escaped) every one, almost, having a *differing Sound*.

82. As this Author seems to have designed a *full stop* at the *Pillar* he hath caused to be erected, and to prevent Travellers

running unaware into that *dangerous* and *dark* Wilderness, caused this Inscription to be put upon it, *viz.*, "Learn what *Diana's Doves* are, which doth vanquish the Lion by ass-waging him; I say, the green Lion, which is indeed the Babylonian Dragon, Killing all things with his Poison. Then at length learn to know the *Caducean Rod* of *Mercury*, with which he works wonders;" *&c.* Therefore I will not step one Step farther without a *Guide*, for I dread going again into the *Labyrinth*.

83. This *Guide* must be a very *wise Man*, endued with singular Gifts; for he must not only tell me the *Interpretation*, but the *Dream itself*; and by this I may judge of his Ability.

84. For, as Kelly saith, "Let no Man lead, unless he knows the Way."

85. Therefore let none mistake my *Enquiring* the Way, for a *Teaching* of it. If any do, and suffer by it, they must blame themselves, not me; for I am *Enquiring*, I say, not *Teaching* the Way. *Masters* cannot be deceived, but *Searchers* may.

86. We do not find this *Enigma* of *Doves* so frequently used as many others, and which also are very difficult to be understood. *These Figures*, I conceive, spring from a Root of Knowledge and Learning, far above the Vulgar's Reach: For, is not this *Art*, saith one, *Kabbalistical*, and *full of Mysteries?* So one of these Masters, well versed in *Rabbinical* Learning, has told us what the name of a *Dove* doth signify, as well as what it doth not, *viz.*:— "The Name of a Dove[53] is *never applied to Metals themselves* (which ought to be well observed by Enquirers, many having erred after this manner) *but the ministering and preparing Natures*. And that he that *understands the Nature of the Burnt Offering* (for Purification) *will not take Turtles themselves, but two young Pigeons* (which are the Off-spring) *or Sons of the Dove*."

87. And this *Secret Pair* he rather appropriates to *Nogah* (Venus) which is the Fifth amongst the Planets; so the Author of *Hermetic Arcanum* calls them the *Birds of Venus*. Though this *Kabbalist* applies the name of *Dove to Diana* also.[54]

88. In the *History of Natural Things,* saith he:– *"Luna* is called the Medicine for the White;[55] because she hath received a Whitening Splendour from the *Sun,* which, by a like shining, illustrates and converts into her own Nature all the Earth, that is the imperfect Metals: And that place of *Isaiah* xxx, 26, may be mystically understood of this, because the Work being finished, she hath got a Solar Splendour.[56] But in that state, the place in *Canticles* vi, 9,[57] belongs to her. But by the same Name the Matter of the Work is called; and so indeed, like to the Horned Moon, she is in the first State of Consistence; and like the full Moon in the last state of Fluidity and Purity."

89. In another place he hath this Passage, speaking of *two Birds,* (which place, I make no doubt, but the Author of *Introitus Apertus* had well considered, if not drawn his early Knowledge from) and of *Argent Vive,* which he calls a Leopard, Water not wetting, and Jordan of the Wise Man, *viz.*:– "And he shall have four Wings of a Bird upon his Back; the four Wings are of two Birds, which exasperate[58] this Beast with their feathers, to the intent he may enter and fight the Lion and the Bear, ... And Power was given him over them, that he may overcome them, and extract their glutinous Blood. Of all these is made one Fourth Beast, which is frightful and terrible and very strong. ... Eating and breaking to pieces himself and others; ... Treading the residue under his Feet."[59]

90. This *Guide* I think may be depended upon, having given Demonstration of his Ability, by telling not only the *Interpretation,* but the *Original figure* itself.

91. More I have not met with in my *Enquiry,* therefore no more can be expected from me concerning this great *Stumbling-block,* at which so many fall into Error.

92. From these things it is very evident, to me, that this Art cannot be found by never so many casual Trials, or Experiments, without a real Knowledge, as Sendivo has written, *viz.*:– "Know for certain also, that this Art is not placed in Fortune, or casual

Invention, but in real Science; and that there is but this one Matter in the World, by which, and of which, the Philosopher's Stone is made, *viz.*, the Mercury of the Philosophers."[60]

93. Out of what this is made, he teaches in his *Treatise of Sulphur*, as well as elsewhere. This is that *Mercury*, saith another, which the returning *Sun* diffuseth everywhere in the *Month of March*, or *House of Aries*; from whence also the Sulphur is to be sought. Which *Sulphur*, in this Work, saith Sendivo, is indeed instead of the *Male*; but the *Mercury* instead of the *Female*; of the Composition and Acting of these two, are generated the *Mercuries of Philosophers*. For as they have a *double Sulphur*, so they have a *double Mercury*, *viz.*, For the *White* and for the *Red*: Which is but seldom, and then very cautiously hinted; and these *Mercuries* differ, both in *Colour* and *Quality*, as may be easily gathered from their Books, by careful Readers.

94. The Author of *Introitus Apertus* indeed hath taught, that there are two Mercuries to the White, used in two different Works; Asserting that the "Actuation of the Mercury for Sol Vulgar, must differ from that of Philosophical Sol." And further, "If (saith he) you shall in your Decoction of *Sol Vulgar*, use the same *Mercury* which is used in our *Sol* (though both flow from the same Root in general) and apply that Regimen of Heat, which the Wise Men in their Books have applied to our Stone, thou art, without all doubt, in an Erroneous Way: And that is the great Labyrinth in which almost all young Practitioners are ensnared. For there is scarce one Philosopher, who in his Writings does not touch both ways."

95. In this, we may say of him, he hath not fallen short of any of them: For he has so interwoven *one* Work with *another*, *one* Regimen with *another*, {and one Fire with another,} (by way of Balance, as I said before, for Discoveries) that little less than the Knowledge of all in Theory, will prevent our falling into constant Error, in some of these particulars; even after the

Field in general is known: and which happened to himself as he confesses, and which I shall mention, as it falls in my Enquiry.

96. These (with many more) are the Difficulties which the Enquirers after this Art have to encounter with; and which, one would think, should rather deter, than encourage, many Men from pursuing it as they do: especially considering the adverse Fortune that attends most Men, who prosecute this Study to their dying Day; finishing their Lives in Ignorance and Despair. This Melancholy Prospect, I say, should leave such a deep Impression upon us, as to make us more cautiously meddle with this rare and difficult Philosophy; which without a *Master* or the special Favour of God, is never attained. As the Author of *The New Light* informs us, *viz.*, "That unless God reveal it by a good Wit, or Friend, it is hardly known."

97. By the *last* most commonly, by the *first* most rarely. For as he adds, *viz.*:– "Though Lully was a Man of a subtle Wit, yet if he had not received the Art from Arnoldus, certainly he had been like those which find it with difficulty; and Arnoldus also received it from a Friend: Every Art and Science is easy to a Master, but not to a Scholar."

98. Therefore this Art is easy to none, though of never so quick a Wit and Parts, but to those that know it only.

99. The *Kabbalist*, I have before mentioned, hath lively prefigured, wise and good Men by *Elisha*; and the foolish Pretenders of this Art, by *Gehazi*, who was indeed Servant to *Elisha*; but to what purpose, the History of them, in the Second Book of *Kings*, showeth.

100. Elisha, an Example of Natural Wisdom, and a Despiser of Riches: He knew how to correct and make wholesome *Poisonous Waters*, and to multiply Treasure beyond the common *Course of Nature*: He could cure the *worst* Infirmities, nay, even raise the *Dead*: He knew *how* and *when* to blind and open the Eyes of Enquirers, also to punish *Mockers*, and even make *Iron* to *swim*; yea, his very Remains were efficacious after he was dead.

101. Gehazi laboured in vain, and remained a Servant for *ever*; never qualified to be a *Master*, notwithstanding he had the Advantage of conversing with so great a one: He was *Covetous, a Liar and Deceiver; a Prattler, boasting of other Men's Deeds*; Conceited and Hasty, thinking he sufficiently understood his Master, when he bids him take his Staff, and lay it upon the Dead Child, presently enterprising, though with an *Heterogeneous Matter*, and so able to effect nothing not discerning the Law of Nature; but *Elisha* applied a *living* Homogenous Agent, and then the Dead was raised. And instead of a double Portion of his Master's Knowledge (which *Elisha* desired and obtained by his Master *Elijah*) Gehazi got a Leprosy, as the Reward of his Doings.

102. A great deal might be observed from this History of Elisha and Gehazi, who are notable Examples of *Wise and Good Men*, and their Reverse, *viz.*, *Foolish* and *Profane*; the last may talk, as Gehazi did, of procuring the *supernatural Son* of the Wise Man, but without being able to effect it; no more can his Successors, which are not a few even at this Day, who not only succeed him in Qualifications but Success.

103. The *Philosophers'* agree with one Voice, that one worthy of this Science must be *strictly Virtuous*, leading a holy Life, or God will not prosper him: He must have a *competent Understanding*, or he will not be able to conceive: He must be *Diligent* and *Laborious*, or he will not be able to work out what he conceives; and he must be *private* or he will not quietly enjoy that which he works out. To these must be added *Patience* and *Leisure*, together with a *Competent Fortune*; which is the more necessary in this Study, because it requires, as is already said the *whole Man* to find out the Means, and then a careful Application is absolutely necessary to accomplish the Work.

104. The *Philosophers*, you very well know, take the liberty of *seemingly* Contradicting themselves, and one another: Sometimes asserting the Work to be *very easy*; other times that

it is very difficult or hard. One while, that it is short; then again that it is *very tedious*. Again, that it is done with *little Expense*, and an *easy Labour*; then complaining of the *Charge* and *Toil*. Sometimes affirming their Matter to be but *one only thing*, other times that it is compounded of *several*. One while the Work is to be done with a *gentle Fire*, another time that it is not performed without a *strong*. Then again, that it is *equal*, and of the *same degree*; and yet that it is *daily increased*.

105. These are the Difficulties with many more that might be Named which *Enquirers* lie under. And yet the *Philosophers* affirm, they all vanish when the Key of this Art is once attained, which is the Chalibs of *Philosophers*. No longer will a Tyro relish a *false Writer*, or be to seek to reconcile *the true*. For that as soon as the *first* Gate is opened, all the rest will fly open of themselves.

106. I fear many will be displeased and say, these difficulties are too well known to us already, we want rather to be told how we shall overcome them, than have them repeated to us. To these I answer, in the Philosopher's Words, "Expound the Philosopher's Writings according to Nature and not to Fancy." Now they say, their *Stone* is nothing else but "Gold digested to the highest degree of Purity and subtle Fixity." Many {may} consent to this but will plead, that *common Gold* is not meant. In answer to which I shall add, let them read Sendivo on the *Elements of Fire, &c.*, the *Way to Bliss*, and others, and consider the *Extensibility, Permanency* and *Purity* of the Gold there spoken of. And also let them consider whether it is not *such Gold* they would produce by this Art, as is called common Gold. Then if it be *common Gold* you would produce, whether common Gold be not the Natural Body for such a Production; as common Man is of producing its own Kind; common Wheat, of Wheat; and so throughout whole Nature.

107. *Common Wheat* in a Barn, is as dead as *common Gold* in a chest; though both these have a Life, *i.e.,* of Existence, and Power to increase their Kind; which Life must die, before the

Power is brought to Action; and when this is done, they are properly called *living Gold*, and *living Wheat*, and not before.

108. Now, how comes Wheat to be so, we are pretty well apprized, *viz.*, it is sown in its *proper Vessel*, the Earth; it is moistened with its *proper Humidity* and it is digested by its *proper Heat*, and so it grows and increases.

109. And if we are to take *Nature* for our Example, Gold must be proceeded with after the same manner; though the Vessel, the Humidity and Heat differ, for a *Metal* and for a *Vegetable*, yet both are liable to the Deficiencies and Excess of these things.

110. For if Wheat hath not a Matrix duly qualified, or hath *too much* or *too little* Humidity, and so of *Heat*, it will succeed accordingly. And so must the other, if Nature be the same in the *one* as in the *other*, as no doubt she is; or to what purpose are we so often recommended to the Consideration of Nature. Sendivo bids us "follow Nature; waving the many Subtleties of the Philosophers," written to amuse the Unskilful Enquirers.

111. To conclude on this Head, if every Multiplication is from *Seed*; that the Perfection of everything is its attaining a *Seminal Virtue*; and that nothing has this, which is *imperfect* of its Kind: Then it will follow, that if there be a *Seminal Virtue* in Metals, and that all of them are of the *same Nature*, the Seminal Virtue (that is the power of Multiplying) can be nowhere but in the *most Perfect*, which is Gold; *vide* Ars Metallica.

112. As these things are consonant to *Nature, Sound Reason* and *the Doctrine of Philosophers*, even the *most envious*, I, for my part, shall make them my Rule in my *Enquiry*: Others may do as they please.

113. And as the Author of the *Way to Bliss* has not only told us (among many others) where the *Seed of Gold* lies, *viz.*, in Gold; but how it lies, *viz.*, "This Seed of Gold is his whole Body loosened and softened in his own Water; there is all your Stuff and Preparation." So he hath also, with the same Candour,

showed us the *Water* in which it *dies*, and with which it is *raised*. Where speaking of the Affinity that is known between *Gold* and *Quicksilver* (in common Uses) which he calls the *grand Mother of the Stone, and Spring of all her Goodness*: Wherefore, says he:— "When this fine and clean Body of Quicksilver is made, by Nature and Art, yet much finer and clearer, and again, as much more piercing and spiritual, and able to perform it; how much more readily will she run to her like, and devour it, the clean, fine and spiritual, that is the Quick silvery part of the Metal. And if she does devour it, then it cannot be lost, but must need to go into a better Nature, even the Nature we desire."

114. This, he says, is done by the well-ordering the *witty Fire of Hermes*:— "that here is all the Hardness, here all the World is blinded all the rest is easy. Search then this rare kind of Heat; for here is all the Cunning; this is the Key of all; this makes the Seeds and bringeth forth: Search wisely, and where it is, in the midst of Heaven and Earth; for it is in the midst of both these places, and yet but one indeed; it is Earthy, yet Watery, Airy, and very Fiery, *&c.* He adds, Let the dew of this starry Blood beat about the Womb, and your Seed shall joy and prosper.—Muse and conjecture well upon my Words, you that are fit and skilled in Nature, for this is a very Natural Heat; and yet all the World is blinded. Nay indeed, if a Man would read little, and think much upon the Ways of Nature, he might easily hit this Art; and before that, never."

115. Thus {has} the witty Author, according to the Custom of all Philosophers, brought us to a full stop, and left us to consider Nature, in order to remove the *Remora*[61] that so often stops Enquirers in their Career.

116. It was from the Excellency and Virtue of this Fire, no doubt, that the *Kabbalist* I have before mentioned intituled his wonderful Book, *Æsch Mezareph, or Purifying Fire.*[62]

117. This Fire has lain hid from many, a long time after they knew the Field in general, where the Seed was to be sown. The

fiery Furnace of Philosophers, says one of them, "lay hid from me long; but after I knew this, and how it was fitted to its proper Vessel, after a few days I beheld the admirable Brightness of our Water, which being seen, I could not but be amazed."

118. So Pontanus seems surprised at the wonderful Effects of this Fire, for want of the Knowledge of which he had erred so long and often; and tells us who informed him of it, *viz.,* Artephius,[63] whose Book is extant, and read by most Enquirers, though not with the same success; some interpreting his Sayings *one way,* and some *another;* but few according to the true Sense and Meaning. Whence they have erred and will always err, unless they learn it better; the way to learn it, is but just told above, by the Author of the *Way to Bliss,* which agrees {exactly} with the "Way" Pontanus prescribes, *viz.,* "They that should read Geber, and all other Philosophers, never so long, could not comprehend it, because that Fire is found by deep and profound Meditation only; and then it may be gathered from Books, and not before."

119. We must not only have the Knowledge of *this* Fire; but, as we are often told, the true *Measure* of it to its *Furnace;* both which seem to be remote from the Eyes of the Vulgar: When this is known, the Difficulties that attend the *Radical Dissolution* of the close and fixed Body of Gold vanish. And before this can be done, this stout fixed Body must be *Calcined,* and reduced into as fine a Calx as possible, which is often hinted by *Philosophers,* but with a design to conceal it. Geber witnesses, that "everything Calcined is of easier Solution, because the Parts of the Calcined Body, more subdilated by Fire, are more easily mixed with Water, and turned into Water." Without this previous Calcination, no Solution is found.

120. Therefore no wonder so many fail in their Attempts, to dissolve Gold in a *Generative* Way, by working on its Compact and *Gross* Body; For as the gross Bodies of *Sol* and *Luna* are not fit for Dissolution, but only their

altered and *unctuous* Calxes; so *Mercury*, in its gross Body, is not able to do this, but in its *altered* more *subtle* and *spiritual* Nature; and drawn from its *Vitriolic Caverns*, actuated with its *pure Salt* and *piercing Sulphur*, which then overcomes all things, even itself. For it not only dissolves *Sol* and *Luna* into its own Nature, but coagulates itself into theirs, *true* and *fixed*, by a proper Heat only.

121. Some may say, All these {things} are so fully taught already, that a bare repeating of them is of no use.

122. That they are taught already, by the *Masters* of this Science themselves, is my warrant for repeating of them; and if you have already Learned these things, you have no Reason to be uneasy; if you have not, it is your advantage to be put in mind of them, even by an *Enquirer*.

123. Sad experience showeth, that but very few of the past or present Searchers, learn those things which they often *brag* the Philosophers have taught: But at length to cover their own Ignorance, they fall into Arrogance, and blame the Philosophers for hiding of them; as is observed by (the never too much to be admired) Candid Ripley; who, in return, only modestly reproves them, Thus:—

"All Philosophers record and say the same;
But simple Searchers putteth them in blame,
Saying, they hide it; But they arc Blame worthy,
Who are no Clerks and meddle with Philosophy."

124. Here this good Man, in *few words*, justifies the true Philosophers, and lays the blame where it ought, *viz.*, on the *Unskilful Meddlers* with Philosophy.

125. What though he has concealed the *Key* of the Art under his *Green Lion*, as others have done under the *Doves, Chalibs, Secret Fire, &c.*, some under one Figure, some under another, which best answered their purpose, *viz.*, "Concealing the Art from the Unworthy." What they have done towards Discovering of it to the Deserving, merits the

greatest Acknowledgements, not Censure from Enquirers to whom they declare they are not indebted.

126. Nor do I affirm, that all these different Terms are synonymous, that behoves the Enquirer to satisfy himself in, from their Writing, whether they are or can be deemed so.

127. I have ventured to call the *Green Lion* of Ripley the *Key* of the Work, because his Expositor has as good as called it so. "Learn then," says he, "to know this Green Lion, and its Preparation, which is all in all the Art; it's the only Knot; untie it, and you are as good as Master: For whatever then remains, is but to know the outward Regimen of the Fire, for to help on Nature's Internal Work."

128. And the *same Author* has expressly called the *Chalibs* so, *viz.*, "I will tell thee (if thou wilt conceive) it is called *Chalibs*, by the Author of the *New Light*;[64] and it is the true Principle of the Work, the true Key (as it may be handled) of unlocking the most hidden Secrets of Philosophers."

129. Again, "Our *Chalibs* is the true Key of our Work, without which the Fire of the Lamp could not be, by any Art, kindled." Which he further describes thus, *viz.*, "It is the Mineral of Gold, a Spirit very pure, beyond others, *&c.*"

130. Sendivogius calls this Matter, as well by the Name of *Magnet*, as *Chalibs*, *viz.*, "To speak more plainly," says he, "it is our *Magnet*, which, in our foregoing Treatises, I called *Chalibs*, or Steel. The Air generates this Magnet, and the Magnet generates or makes out Air to appear and come forth: I have here entirely showed thee the Truth."

131. This Author has comprised in *few Words* what the Author of *Introitus Apertus* has divided into Three Chapters, *viz.*, *Chalibs*, *Magnet*, and *Air*; all which he has Concentrated in a Fourth, *viz.*, *Chaos*. "The Earth," says he, "is a heavy Body, the Matrix of Minerals, because it keeps them occultly in itself; although it brings to light Trees and Animals. The Heaven is that wherein the great Lights,

together with the Stars, are roiled about; and it sends down its Virtues through the Air into inferior things."

132. When he has gone thus far, he, in Imitation of Sendivogius's Skill and Candour, adds, "But in the Beginning, all being confounded together, made a *Chaos*. Behold! I have faithfully opened to you the Truth; for our *Chaos, &c.*"

133. O the Harmony and Skill, as well as Candour of these two great Masters! Beg of God that he would make you Discerners and Partakers of these things. Nor let me forget most candid Ripley, who exactly corresponds with these, *viz.*:—

"For as of one Mass was made all things,
Right; so must {it} in our Practice be.
In Philosophers Books therefore, who lifts to see,
Our Stone is called the less World One and Three:
Magnesia also of *Sulphur*, and *Mercury*,
Proportionate by Nature most perfectly."

134. Thus we see Ripley's *One Mass*, Philalethes's *Chaos*, and Sendivogius's *Matter of the Antient Philosophers*, are the same; containing Three, *viz.*, *Magnet, Chalibs, Air*, or *Magnesia, Sulphur* and *Mercury*: Which also are called by abundance of other Names in Philosophers' Books, *e.g.*, Artephius speaking of the Compound, *Magnesia*, says, "That it is compounded,[65] like a Man of Body, Soul and Spirit;" which he thus expounds, *viz.*:— "For the Body is the fixed Earth of the Sun, which is more than most fine, ponderously lifted up by the force of our Divine Water: The Soul is the Tincture of the Sun and Moon, proceeding from the Conjunction or Communication of these two: But the Spirit is the Mineral Virtue of the Two Bodies and the Water, which carries the Soul, *&c.*" Again, "The Spirit therefore pierceth, the Body fixeth, the Soul coupleth, coloureth and whiteneth. Of these three united together, is our Stone made; that is, of the Sun, and Moon, and Mercury. Flamel says, he could easily give very clear Comparisons and Expositions of this Body, Soul and Spirit: But then he must

of necessity speak things which God reserves to reveal unto them that fear and love him, and consequently ought not to be written;" yet be is not wanting to concur with Artephius, in calling them the *Sun, Moon* and *Mercury*, and agreeing exactly with him in his Exposition.

135. It would be as it were endless, and indeed needless, to recite all the different Expressions used by Philosophers, who confirm and constantly maintain this Doctrine of Trinity in Unity, under various modes of Speech, and hard-to-be-understood Similes.

136. But to keep a little to that of the *Green Lion*, which is worth our Enquiry: Ripley speaking of its *Blood*, asserts this Secret to be hid by all Philosophers, *viz.*:—

> "The said Menstrual is (I say to thee in Counsel)
> The Blood of our Green Lion, and not of Vitriol:
> Dame Venus can the Truth of this thee tell
> At the beginning, to Counsel if thou her call.
> This Secret is hid by Philosophers great and small.
> Which Blood, drawn out of the Green Lion,
> For lack of Heat, had not perfect Digestion."

137. So the Author of the *Hermetic Arcanum* saith, "the most precious Substance is Venus, the Hermaphrodite of the Antients, glorious (or powerful) in its double Sex."

138. The Author of *Æsch Mezareph,* speaking of Venus, under the Names *Nogah* and *Hod,* "which is a necessary Instrument to promote the Metallic Splendour," says, "It has more a part of a Male, than Female; and speaking of the Green Lion," he saith, "Which, I pray thee, do not think is called so from any other Cause but its Colour: For unless thy Matter shall be green, not only in that immediate State before it is reduced into Water, but also after the Water of Gold is made of it." Why it is called a *Lion*, is hinted by another, *viz.*, "Having Power to overcome, and reduce

Bodies to their first Matter, and to make fixed things volatile and spiritual; whence it is fitly called a *Lion*."

139. Some there are who derive the Name *Green* from the Rawness or Unripeness of the Subject, and not from the Colour, *viz*.:—

"Whose Colour doubtless is not so,
And that your Wisdom does well know;
But our Lion wanting Maturity,
Is called *Green*, from Unripeness, trust me."
                                    The Hunting of the Green Lion.

140. Another says:—

"For it is because of its transcendent Force
It hath, and for the Rawness of its Source,
Of which the like is nowhere to be seen,
That it of them is named their *Lion Green*.
Our subject is no ways malleable;
It is Metalline, and its Colour sable."
                                    Sophic Feast.

141. These are some more of the *seeming* Contradictions, which Philosophers warn us not to be deceived with, but to learn to Reconcile. These Difficulties are to be overcome by Meditation only.

142. Now, let us try whether, or how far, it is possible to Reconcile these Contradictions concerning the *Green Lion*. The *Kabbalist* (much admired by me) says, the Matter is *actually green*, both before it is dissolved and afterwards also: This doth not deny, but confirm, that it is spoke of, and considered, in divers States; and then it may not be absurd to suppose, that it may be, and is, described by *one* in one state and degree of Perfection, and by *others* in another: By one in its *Impurity*; by another in its Passage from thence to its *Purity* (for Ripley says it is unclean); and by a third when it is *Purified*. For as Matters, when more or less pure or mature, are of a different Texture,

so they also differ in Colour. And it is in this Sense, I make no doubt the Philosophers are to be understood, not only with relation to this Subject, but {in their other Doctrines also.} It is not therefore every Matter which is *foul* or *green* (as Vitriol is, which Ripley says, Fools take to be their *Green Lion*) that entitles it to this wonderful Name; no, but it must have all the other *Virtues* and *Powers* in it, that are assigned by Philosophers: Which thing lies very obscure, and seemingly base, but it is, in its Purity and exalted Virtue, their *Subject of Wonders*. To produce which, this *foul Minera*,[66] they tell us, must be *dissolved* and *exactly purified*, in a pure Homogeneal Water, which is its own *Blood*, as White as Milk; which Name some have rather imposed. This *Leprous Body*, Sendivo and others have called *Saturn*, and *Saturn's Child*; and what some have called *Blood* and *Milk*, he calls *Urine*.

143. Thus the Masters of this Science take the liberty to express themselves by different Similes, in order to disguise their Secret, which a mental Man will discover and improve by, as soon as he shall discern any one of their Intentions; the rest follow in course, though varied ever so many ways, as they themselves testify.

144. What some have called *Blood, Wine, &c.*, the Author of the *Learned Sophics Feast* calls *fiery Water, &c., viz.:*—[67]

> "Their Lion Green they suffer'd him to prey
> On *Cadmus* Sociates; and when the Fray
> Was over, they with Dian's charms him ty'd
> And made him under Waters to abide,
> And wash'd him clean; and after gave him Wings
> To fly, much like a Dragon, whose sharp Springs
> Of fiery Water, the only way was found
> To cause *Apollo* his Harp-strings to sound.
> This is the true Nymph's Bath, which we did try,
> And proved to be the Wise Men's Mercury."

145. Here all *Doubts* and *Difficulties* end, when this is attained; so with it I shall finish this *Enquiry*: Having showed my Fellow Enquirers, in what manner I have been entertain'd[68] in it; concluding in the Words of the aforesaid Author, *viz.*:—

> "Happy are they, who shall not miss to find
> The new uprising Sun:[69]
> More happy they, who, with renewed Mind,
> In God find Rest alone."

The SHORT

ENQUIRY

Concerning the

Hermetick Art

(Which was Printed with the
Latin and *Englisſh*

Æſch-Mezareph)

CONTINUED.

By a Lover of Philaletha.

PART II.

LONDON:
Printed in the Year 1715.

The Hermetic Art, Part II was first published in 1715, by a anonymous printer, London.

This edition was published by The Golden Dawn Research Trust in 2013.

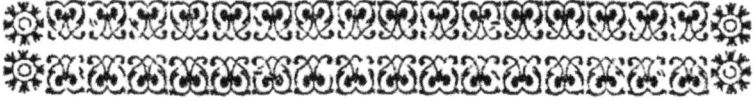

THE HERMETIC ART.[70]

————∘∘⟡∘∘————

PART II.

J UST as I was finishing this short Enquiry, I heard, as it were, many Voices hastily crying, Hold on, *Investigator*, do not leave us yet! All thou hast hitherto said will signify nothing to us, unless some further Explanation be made; for our Doubts are as many, and as strong as before.

2. *Investigator*. How, Gentlemen! I am sorry for that; I was in hopes that this candid Recapitulation (for so it is) of the Doctrine of the Philosophers, would either have made you altogether decline this Search, or else to have proceeded more regularly in it. But as your Numbers are great, it is too difficult a Task for me to suit my Discourse to every one of your Capacities and Notions. Therefore it may be more proper to hear your several Wants and Complaints: which happily you may supply and redress out of the Magazine of your own Cogitations and Experiments.

3. For although every one of you want the Knowledge of some one thing, yet your Wants not being alike, who knows, I say, but every one may be supplied by each other's Labours and Study?

4. And for the better Dispatch and more orderly Proceeding, let as many as are of one Mind, appoint one to speak for them, under their several Classes, beginning with the first Letter of the Alphabet, and so on to the last; and if there are not Letters enough, begin with the Numerical Numbers, which probably may hold out: Let A begin.

5. A. For my part, and those I represent, I can now tell you, that after much Study, and a Multitude of Erroneous Experiments, our Theory is settled to our Satisfaction. This I take to be a great Point gained; especially to find it so well Founded, and so authentically Confirmed, by some of the Authors.

6. We find, it is by the Air, and Heavenly Influences attending it, that all things are enlivened and subsist. This is excellently hinted by Sendivo, *viz.*:— "There is in the Air a secret Food of Life, which in the Night we call *Dew*, and in the Day *Rarefied Water*, whose invisible Congealed Spirit is better than all the Earth."[71]

7. We must therefore find out a Subject, in which this Invisible Spirit is corporified. Now we think, that the same Author has as candidly Named that, *viz.*:— "O our Nitre, and wonderful *Salt-Petre!*"[72] This is plain Doctrine, and admits of no dispute. Nor is it a Wonder that so many have erred working on *May-Dew, Rain-Water, &c.* before this Spirit is congealed into this wonderful Body; and by which it is brought, through Coagulation, nearer a Mineral Nature, as you may observe in its Fusion; its parts are so uniform, that it defends the Spirit in the Fire; for unless the Body be divided by a Bole, or takes Fire, the Spirit flies not. Nor can we doubt, but this has Relation to what the same Author has said, *viz.*:— "Take that which is, but does not appear till it is the Artificer's pleasure. This is, The Universal Spirit is in this Subject, but appears not till the Artificer makes it appear by Distillation, and which we know is then a Powerful Dissolvent."[73]

8. Now the only difficulty that remains to us, is how to do this, so as to destroy its Corrosive and preserve its Dissolving Nature, that it might act upon the Bodies without Corrosion; that is, in his own Words, "Dissolve *Sol* as sweetly as Ice dissolves in warm Water."[74] All the rest is so easy, that one could scarce miss if one would.

9. B. There is a certain matter, which was created by God, and is common to all, and likewise to be had without cost, at least very little; but this not equally good, some being abundantly more filled with the Universal Spirit than other; this being handled according to Art, yields a Liquor (besides the Phlegm) which some call *Mercurius Duplicatus*, because it contains the White and the *Red Mercury*, and which may easily be separated; these are not Corrosive, but very Friendly to all Bodies, even Vegetable and Animal, and which will not act upon Metals in their Corporeal Forms, so well as it will on their Salts, according to *Johann Isaac Hollandus*.

10. I omitted to tell you two Notable Signs, mentioned by most Philosophers, which is, that in its Distillation, a white Fume with a Stinking Smell are known.

11. Now in the *Caput Mortuum* or Earth that remains, (which you know is often talked of too) there is a precious Salt; this must carefully, according to Art, be extracted with its own Phlegm, and made very pure, and which will succeed the better, if the Phlegm be first rectified. These things accord exactly with the Philosopher, *viz*.:—

"The true Elixir if thou wilt make,
Earth out of Earth look that thou take."

12. Again,

"Take Earth of Earth, Earths Mother,
And Water of Earth, it is no other."[75]

13. Another also saith,

"Earth out of Earth, and Cleansed pure,
By Earth of himself, by [knowing] his Nature."[76]

14. This we think is as plain as words can make it, and which sufficiently satisfies us, not only of the Matter, but Operation. And then these three Principles are again to be intimately united and fixed; which, this Author says, will quickly be done, *viz*.:—

"Then into Purgatory she must be do,
And have the Pains that 'long thereto,
'Till she be brighter than the Sun,
For then thou hast the Mastery won.
And that shall be within Hours three,
The which forsooth is great ferly."[77]

15. This we must own, as he says, is very strange, and what I have not yet been able to effect, no, not in three Months, especially to that Fixity and Weight, which they all talk of, and this Author affirms, *viz.*:—

"Heavy as Metal shall it be,
In which is hid great privity."[78]

Now the only thing we are at a loss in, is, whether it does not require a Calx of Gold to be added before Putrefaction, in order to determine it to Metals. For Noble Sendivo has positively asserted, that if we had the first Matter, yet it would be impossible to multiply the Central Salt, without Gold; which ought to be taken good Notice of.

16. C. A Gentleman, of my Acquaintance, assures me, that a Friend of his told him, he had succeeded to the White, though as yet but of small Virtue, not above one upon twenty; but he is going on to carry it higher: it was a Process upon *Vitriol*.

17. He first dissolved it in distilled Vinegar, and made fair Crystals; which Work he repeated so often, 'till it yielded no foul Sulphur, and then became exquisitely fine; then with a certain *Menstruum* (which his Friend had not yet told him, and in which the greatest Secret lay) he putrefied in the Cold, and afterwards with a proper Bole distilled it.

18. First, There came a Phlegm, and when the white Fumes began to come, he changed the Receiver, which was very clean and dry, and strongly luted it; these Fumes continued about two Days and Nights, and afforded much delight, by their Roilings in the Receiver; when they ceased, the Fire was urged to the highest degree, for Four and Twenty Hours, which brought

over a small quantity of *Red Oil*, and from the *Caput Mortuum* (after an open Calcination) was extracted a pure fixed Salt, with distilled *May-Dew*. He then, according to Art, separated the White from the Red Oil, which was very ponderous and fiery. The Salt was put into an Egg, and imbibed with the White Oil (the proportion not told him) which he putrefied, whitened and fixed, and then fermented with a Calx of *Luna*, and so projected.

19. And for the Red, it was to be imbibed with the Red Oil, and fermented with *Sol*.

20. Now the only thing that I want, is the knowledge of the *Menstruum*, which will purify the Crystals in the Cold, and of which should be glad to be informed.

21. D. A very Ingenious Friend of mine, who has been hard upon this Study for many years, has now so contrived a Furnace, as will give all the degrees of Heat imaginable at the same time. He says, There is no Subject in the World, but he could work in it. The Apartments are so numerous, and so admirably contrived, that it would puzzle even a Philosopher to find out their several Uses. I own, every time I see it, I cannot but stand amazed at the Contrivance.

22. By the help of this Furnace, he proposes to try more Experiments in a Month, than other ways he could do in Ten. It is not to be thought, the Errors he has already discovered in Practice, and goes on with great exactness daily to discover more. If he holds on, he may come up to the Numbers of Ripley's, *Trevison*, or any of them all; and consequently cannot be long e're he overtakes them in Truth; for when all the Errors are worked up, nothing else will be left.

23. He has already likewise arrived at a Demonstration, that not one of the Subjects that have been used for the *Doves of Diana*, by the great Numbers of Operators in *Germany, France, &c.* has been the right. But he does not question, but by the help of this Furnace, in a very little time, to be able to say more about them.

24. Now he having offered me, that if I, or any Friend of mine, have any likely Matter to propose for this obscure pair of Birds, he would soon let me know the Success, and it should not cost a Farthing. For you must know, he is employed by a Rich Man to find out Errors in Practice, in order to make a Catalogue of them, as other Philosophers have done. But I fear it will not be compleat, for he Regifters only the capital ones, the rest he thinks he shall remember.

25. Now I am at a great stand what Subject to propose to him, which has not been found already to be false, and that bears their Characteristics. For they must not be any Poisonous Matter, but on the contrary, they must have Healing under their Wings, with which they contemporate the Malignity of the Air.

26. They must not be any common thing, because no Eye but a true Philosopher's ever saw them. They must not be any foul thing, because they are said to have *pure Silvery-wings*, and *Shining-bright Attire*.

27. And yet they must not be Metals themselves, because the Author of *Æsch Mezareph,* asserts it, which is known to be a woeful Truth to many.

28. I therefore freely own, I know not what Subject or Matter, that is anyways promising, to recommend to the Trial: In this one thing I would gladly be informed, that I might not lose so good an opportunity of having it done for nothing.

29. *Investigator.* Note, This has been a very large Class, but are, through Disappointments, &c. much dwindled.

30. D. As for our parts, after all other Considerations, we can never believe, but that the Subject of this Great Work must be in the Mineral Kingdom alone. Though on the other hand, we cannot but consent to the Opinion, that common Metals melted in the Fire cannot affect it. For the Philosopher has told us, "That the Fire of *Vulcan* is the Artificial Death of the Metals; and that as many as have suffer'd Fusion, have in it lost their Life."[79]

31. Therefore our firm Opinion is, that there is a certain Matter to be chosen in this Kingdom, "not yet perfected by Nature, nor yet perfected by Nature, nor yet totally imperfect, but in the way to Perfection."[80] This is such a Matter as the Author of the *Hermetic Arcanum or Secrets* recommends, "that has Life and Spirits in it, not extinct, as those that are handled of the Vulgar. For who can expect Life from Dead Things?" If this Living Matter could be found, we make no doubt, but that (as we are told) the Work would be the most Expeditious of any, as well as of greatest Perfection. We hope therefore we may have some *Light* given us of this one Matter, and its Preparation, resolving not to trouble our Heads about many, whatever any shall say to the contrary.

32. E. There is a Person that has been in pursuit of these things a long time, who has now found a way to produce *Sol* and *Luna* from Quicksilver; Copper, and other Ingredients, by a short Digestion; he only wants to know how to fix them, that is, so as to abide the Test; for other ways, they seem fixed enough. Now he has offered me, that if I can put him in a way to do this, he will tell me all the rest of the Process. Therefore if I could be instructed in this one thing, I will content myself with this Particular.

33. *Investigator.* I thank you, Gentlemen, who have at present declared your Opinions, for the Return you have made, by letting me see likewise, in what manner you have been entertained in your Enquiry: Upon all which I have this to say, It is no new thing to find many Men of many Minds; nor does it fare worse with you, than it did with Enquirers in Ripley's time, who has Recorded of them, that "what for the more, and what for the less, evermore something wanting there was."

34. Therefore be of good Cheer; unite your Counsels, wet your Wits, and exert your several Talents; and who knows what may yet be done? The Philosophers, it is true, are crafty, but you much outdo them in Numbers. Join your Purses and your

Skill, and what Difficulty can stand before you? What hard Sayings can obstruct your Knowledge?

35. I will go on to assist you, according to the meanness of my Capacity. Strike the Flint upon the Steel, and make the Sparks fly about briskly; illuminate the Darkness, which is one degree of Perfection; banish the Clouds, which obnubilate your Understandings. Cease not until you have made the Light of a Star as the Light of the Moon, the Light of the Moon as the Light of the Sun, and the Light of that as the Light of seven Days. Thus go on to multiply Light in a proper Subject, and the Stone is at hand.

36. Now this must first be done at home; that is, have you one Spark of Light in your Heads, add more, till there is not a dark Corner in them, even until they are, as it were, Diaphanous. Don't go on to multiply Darkness, by adding one whimsical Fancy to another; but to the real Knowledge of one thing, add the real Knowledge of another; or else stand still, and rest in the Knowledge of the first thing. Folly darkens Knowledge, as Knowledge enlightens and dissipates Folly, and as Day does Night. *Pride not thyself in thy Folly*; that is, do not boast of Knowledge, whilst ignorant: Confess thy Ignorance, and be humble; and remember the Fate of those two antient Enquires in Sendivo who were despised and laughed at by Nature, for their Confidence.

37. This Manifestation, or Multiplication of Light, is much Celebrated by all Philosophers; "These Words" (says one of them) "are sufficient for a Son of Art," *viz.,* "And Darkness was upon the face of the Deep. And the Spirit of the Lord moved upon the Waters; and God said, Let there be Light, and there was Light; the Light he called Day, and the Darkness Night."[81]

38. A. That Author does indeed say so, but he means to the Adept Sons of Art, not for such Tyro's as we. For we can bear Witness, those words are not sufficient for us, whatever he or any Body else may say.

39. *Investigator.* You had better invert your saying, and there will need no Controversy about it. That is, that you are not sufficient for those things; which is truly the Case. Contend not with the Philosophers, for though your Numbers are much the greater, yet their Harmony will be too strong for your Disagreements, which renders you weak.

40. D. I think, by this Discourse, those of my Mind, may have some Light, for though we are not sufficient for everything, for I told you, wherein I was at a stand, yet we Understand several things well, and particularly this *Chaos* has been pretty plain to us for many Years. Concerning which, I have this to say; I know how to bring a certain dark Matter, to the brightness of a Star, and which you will say is a good Step. And as the Stars you read, were created on the Fourth Day, so is this on the Fourth Operation, which I esteem as a very great Secret, and which I never told to anyone before. I wish I knew the Fifth Day's Work as well, wherein the Birds, or winged Fowls were made; and this I take to be a good degree of Knowledge, though not a competent one.

41. *Investigator.* How far this will appear to be any degree of Knowledge, farther than is known to everyone that reads the History of the Creation, will be known best to yourselves, who know, if any Body does, your further Intentions on this *Body of Light*, if you will allow me to call it a Body, for it may be you think a higher Appellation is due to it. But if it be the true *Chaos* of Philosophers, and if theirs bears an Analogy with the Antient, it not only contains in it the Sun, Moon and Stars, but the whole Heavens and the Earth, and all things contained therein. And it seems to me highly improbable, that any Men should be skilful in the first Four Days work, and remain ignorant of the other two. Therefore my advice is, review your Notion, and consider whether there be any Weight in what I say. For either you have not the true *Chaos*, or you have all things actually contained in it, as in the beginning; or else I

have not a right Notion of a *Chaos*. Nor had I needed to have added this, if you had observed my Opinion, delivered before and grounded upon *Ripley*, *viz.*, "For as of one Mass was made all things," (*viz.*, in the great World) "right so, must it in our Practice be."[82] That is, just so must it be in our Work. Now at what time, this must be in their Work, as at the Creation of the World, the first Words in *Genesis* sufficiently showeth, *viz.*, "In the Beginning," &c. which is also confirmed by the Philosopher I quoted in the former Part of this Enquiry, *viz.*, speaking of the Heavens, with the Sun, Moon and Stars, and the Earth with the Minerals, &c. it produceth. "But in the Beginning, all being confounded" (Promiscuously mixed) "together, made a *Chaos*. Behold! I have Religiously showed you the Truth."[83]

42. Therefore yourselves may judge, whether the Subject you propose to yourselves, is the *Chaos* whereof the Philosophers write, or not. That is, If it actually contains their Heaven and Earth, and likewise their Sea, and consequently their Sun, Moon and Stars, theirs Minerals, Fishes, &c. it is their *Chaos*; if not, it is not theirs. Have a care therefore of making a false Step in this beginning; if you do, every Step afterwards goes on to multiply Errors, but will never multiply Metals. However let my Opinion of these things merit no greater Authority with you than it deserves, though candidly given by me, always preferring Masters themselves.

43. B. I am sure the Matter I mentioned to you before, and the Practice too, agrees with these things, and I think we have great Encouragement to proceed, since it appears to me to be the Matter, for it contains everything in itself, both Minerals, Metals, and even Mercury, as well as Precious Stones; and where, I pray, will you find such another Subject in the whole World?

44. *Investigator*. If what you say be true, it comes pretty near indeed, that which a Philosopher had said of their *Chaos*, and

one that is not of the least Authority with me, *viz.*, "Although in itself it be wholly Volatile, all the Metals may be drawn out of it without the transmuting *Elixir*; even *Sol* and *Luna*, also *Mercury*."[84] Therefore if your Matter contains all these things in it, nothing remains for you to do, but to draw them out, and be Rich.

45. B. I could really prove to you, if I might without discovering the matter, that the Subject we speak of, not only contains in itself these things, but they are continually drawn out of it, by Men skilled in it, in divers parts of the World. And as I am promised acquaintance with some of these Artists, I shall closely press after it, when my time will permit me.

46. *Investigator.* You do well to be first at leisure; for as the Philosopher has said:— "Those that are in Public Honours and Offices, or be always busied with Private and Necessary Occupations, let them not strive to attain to the top of this Philosophy. For that he ought to have little to do with the World, abstaining from Company, and enjoy constant Tranquillity, that the Mind may be able to Reason more freely in Private, and be higher lifted up, in order to penetrate the hidden Mysteries of Truth."[85]

47. The same Philosopher has made another very true, though Melancholy Observation, *viz.*:— "The Alchymists, who have given their Minds to their, well-nigh, innumerable Sublimations, Distillations, &c. more subtle than profitable, and so have distracted them by variety of Errors, as so many Tormentors, that they never will be bent again, by their own Genius, to the plain Way of Nature and Light of Truth, from whence their industrious Subtlety has declined them, and by Twinings and Turnings, as by the *Lybian* Quicksands, hath drowned their entangle Wits; The only hope of Safety remaining, in finding a faithful Guide and Teacher, that may make the shining Sun conspicuous to them, and vindicate their Eyes from Darkness."[86]

48. If I could entertain you with anything of my own, which is what you seem to expect, that was more Valuable, I should not be wanting; but since this good Man, and one of the greatest Philosophers, has said so much for your Instruction, suffer me to put you in mind of a few more of his curious Cautions; and as they cannot be outdone, so they will not fail to have a good Effect where they are truly embraced.

49. "Let a Student of this Secret carefully avoid Reading or keeping Company with false Philosophers; for nothing is more dangerous to a Learner, in any Science, than the Company of an Unskilful or Deceitful Wit, by which false Principles are stamped for true, whereby an honest or too credulous a Mind is seasoned with bad Doctrine. Let a Lover of Truth make use of few Authors, but of best Note and experienced Truth. Let him suspect things, which are quickly understood, especially in Mystical Names and Secret Operations; for Truth lies hid in Obscurity. Nor do Philosophers ever write more Deceitfully, then when Plainly; nor even more truly, then when Obscurely."[87]

50. I know you think it lost time to repeat these Shining Truths, with which I am greatly delighted, pleading you have read all these things already; I heartily wish you had not only read them, but made them your own by Practice and Experience, which I too well know most Men neglect to do, and fare accordingly.

51. And as there is not time enough now to go through the Alphabet, it being very Dark, and near Midnight, let us adjourn to Sun-rising; for this Study requires a better Light than we now partake of.

52. A, B, C, &c. Good, Mr. *Investigator*, don't let us part without a Process, for that is all in all with us; we think our time ill spent, if about anything else; all other talk Confounds rather than Instructs us.

53. *Investigator*. I am not of your Mind, for I take a free Reasoning about the Theory to be more profitable; for want of a Competent Knowledge of which, you can neither Form any True Process, nor discern one that is already Formed. There is no Similitude between those you have mentioned, or can mention of such like Operations, and the Philosophical. For as the true Matters of Philosophers differ from every vulgar Matter, so their Manner of Operating differs from all such vulgar Ways of Proceeding.

54. You, I think, know I do not speak these things of myself, or alone, but all of them affirm, that their Furnace, Fire and Vessel, as well as their Water, Earth and Air, yea, everything else that is theirs, are not only not vulgar, but were never seen by them, nor ever will be.

55. These things being considered, of what Profit would it be even to hear Processes from the Mouths of Philosophers themselves, whilst we remain Ignorant of the things, whereof they discourse, and take the Vulgar for them?

56. However to gratify your Expectations and eager Desires, I shall communicate a Process, which a very wise Man related to me; but at the same time, I must own, and I doubt not but you will concur with me, that it is as hard to reconcile, or be understood, as any you have read in the Philosophers Books. But to proceed, There is, *said he*, a certain Mineral Earth or Body, which is indeed an Anonymous Substance prepared with great Skill, which being reduced into very fine Powder (for it is Frangible) the finer the better, though it will not be so bright as it was before it was reduced into Powder. Which being exactly calcined in a proper Vessel, and by a gentle heat, like that of the *Sun in Pisces* (which will take up sometime, but that must be dispensed with) it will become such a Calx, as will of itself relent, though in a close Room, into a glutinous and heavy Water, such is its immediate alliance with the Air; and the most proper season for this, is in the Month of *March*, the Sun being then in *Aries*.

57. This Water being gently and by degrees distilled, will be very Splendid, yea every Distillation or Cohobation more Splendid then other, till at length it will leave no Impurity in the bottom, though at first there seemed a great deal, but the whole will be turned into Purity, (which he said was a known Truth to all true Philosophers) and he further said, with most Solemn Protestations, that the shortest and easiest way to make the white Sulphur of Philosophers, was by this Water alone in a proper Vessel, and convenient heat only. Believe it, said he, who will, and disprove it who can, it is what I not only know to be true but the greatest Truth.

58. He also said, that this was what *Sendivogius* meant, when he said, *viz.*:— "If thou art Ignorant of this, and knowest not how to boil Air, without all doubt thou shalt Err, seeing this is the matter of the Antient Philosophers.—The receptacle of the Vegetable Seed is the Earth, the receptacle of the Animal Seed is the Womb of the Female, the receptacle of Water, which is the Mineral Seed, is the Air.—In this Element is included the Spirit of the most High.—God hath adorned this Element with the vital Spirit of every Creature.—For as the Loadstone draws to itself Iron" (after the manner of the Arctic Pole drawing Water to itself) "so the Air by a Vegetable Magnetic Power, which is in the Seed, draws to itself the Nourishment of the *Menstruum* of the World."[88] I do assure you, *said this wise Man*, if thou canst once make this Magnet, thou wilt find it so obvious, and so easy to be understood, in the Philosophers Books, that thou wilt stand in need of but little, if any, instruction, to accomplish thy desire.

59. Thus your Importunity has extorted from me the utmost, I have met with in my Enquiry, and I wish this Process may be better understood, and more profitably enjoyed by you than at present, there is any appearance of. And whether what is said by *Norton*, may favour this Process or not, I shall not Determine, but leave to your Consideration, *viz.*:—

"In the Book of *Turba Aristeus* deposed
How Air in Water was secretly enclosed;
Which bear up Earth, with his Airey might,
Pythagoras said, that was spoke with right.
Aristotle, craftily his words set he,
Saying, *Cum habueris ab Aere.*
Plato wrote full sapiently,
And named it, *Stilla roris madidi,*
Which was kindly spoken for Alchemy."[89]

60. Again,

"And Air also with his Coaction,
Makes things to be of easy Liquefaction.

...

And clear Brightness in Colours fair.
Is caused of Kind, evermore of Air."[90]

61. I own these Sayings are very Obscure, and far from plain Discoveries, but let us here remember what was said above, *viz*.:– "Nor do they ever speak more truly, than when Obscurely."[91]

62. I always persuade myself, that where ever we find so many great Philosophers join together in the same Assertion, it is not for nought, but on the contrary, I conclude, there is some great Truth couched in few Words. Here's no less than Aristeus, Pythagoras, Aristotle, Plato and Norton, concurring in Theory and Practice, with the Process I have related to you, and from whence it is not unreasonable to conclude, there is more Truth in it, than may be at first conceived. And who shall determine? Surely he that understands, not he that does not, their Dark Sayings, Parables and Ænigma's; as Norton wittily and merrily has expressed it, *viz*.:–

"For it would be a wondrous thing, and quaint,
A Man that never had Sight to Paint."[92]

63. And you will, I believe, join with him in this true Saying, though you hardly can in another, and retain what you think at present, *viz.*:— "That there are divers shorter, and more inferior ways of making *Gold* and *Silver*, than by the Grand Medicine of the Wise Men;"[93] and may think you have very good grounds for it too, which I am not about to dispute, nor shall I determine whose Authority is best, leaving that to the success. I shall content myself with the bare recital of his Words, reserving my own Opinion to another Opportunity; his Words are these:—

"But to make Silver or Gold is no Engine, *i.e.*, device. Except only the Philosophers Medicine."[94]

64. These things I leave to your Consideration, that have declared your Opinions, as well as with those who are to be heard; not doubting, but as it is your Interest, so you will make it your Business, duly to consider them against our next Meeting, as well as do everything else that will contribute to its being more Profitable than Puzzling. The way to do this, will be to furnish yourselves with Authorities, confirm them by Practice, speak Nature's Language, and your own Experience, not other Men's Tattle.

The Short

ENQUIRY

Concerning the

Hermetick Art

(Which was Printed with the
Latin and *Engliſh*

Æſch-Mezareph)

CONTINUED.

By a Lover of Philaletha.

PART III.

LONDON:
Printed in the Year 1715.

The Hermetic Art, Part III was first published in 1715, by a anonymous printer, London.

This edition was published by The Golden Dawn Research Trust in 2013.

THE HERMETIC ART.[95]

PART III.

INVESTIGATOR. I Hope, Gentlemen, you are come prepared for a Profitable Debate; I can assure you, for my own part, it is for that end and no other I make my Appearance.

2. A. Since our last Meeting, we have considered of it amongst ourselves, and do conclude it will be too little purpose to proceed by showing more of our Intentions, since you neither approve of the Processes already mentioned by us, nor tell us wherein they are amiss. Pray wherein do you think that of ours was so, since it seems to be grounded so firmly on the plain Sayings of the Philosophers I mentioned?

3. *Investigator.* The seeming Authority any Process may have from the Philosophers Books does by no means sufficiently prove it to be right; because as they have called their Matters after the Names of most things which are known, so it is an easy thing to find, in their Books, Names and Expressions which may seemingly favour, I say, almost every Undertaking of this kind, so many are their Allusions, Similes, Metaphors and Parables. I shall therefore make my Replies to you, with as much Philosophical Authority as I may; and in order to it, shall in a very great degree, keep to the Words of the Masters of this Art, though not always to the exact Transcription of them. I shall also Premise, that when I use only a single Authority, it is

for Brevity, or that I think it sufficient; for of this be assured, that I could confirm these with the common consent of all true Philosophers; but a Word to Wise Men is enough, and never so many to the Otherwise would not reform them.

4. In Objection then to your Process upon *Nitre*, as well as to all of the same Kind, varied ever so many ways after the different Fancies of Operators, let this suffice, *viz.*:– Those who seek the Art in Salts, Alloms and Borax's, shall not, nor cannot find it in them. Therefore "it would be a foolish and vain thing, to think to extract the Elixir from anything wherein it is not, as some Infatuated Men have conceited, for that was never the Intention of Philosophers, when they have spoken of such things by Similitude."[96]

5. A. I told you our design was to make only the true Dissolvent from it, whereby we might dissolve *Sol* radically, in order to multiply its Specie; and we think, *Philalethes*, whose Writings you seem to defend, at least Stile yourself a Lover of, approves of such a *Menstruum*.

6. *Investigator*. His Writings do not stand in need of any defence of mine; what I do, in respect to him, is for the sake of others, by showing, and which is unquestionably true, that what he practiced and wrote was Consonant (though by the difference of his way of Writing it may seem to some otherwise) to the Principles and Universal Practice of all the Antient from *Hermes* to this Day; a great Number of whom he quotes, and always to the purpose, some of which I shall Name, though not in order of time, but as they occur, *viz.*:– "Hermes, Morien, Rafis, Albertus, Geber, Artephius, Haly, Rozinus, Arnoldus, Aristotle, Menabdes, Scala Philosophorum, Ludus Puerorum, Arislaus, Guido, Turba, Rosary, Dionysius Zacharius, Bacon, Sendivogius, Lully, Trevisan, Flamel, Hermeticum Arcanum, Johannes de Laznioro, Ripley, Lamsprint, Norton, Richardus, Alanus, Jadocus Greverius, Pontanus, John Mechungus, with many others." But to proceed;

7. Radical Dissolution, in order to Generation or Multiplication of a Species, must be alone performed by the *Radical Humidity of that thing*, which not only dissolves, but adheres and coalesces with it, "but Spirits which are drawn from Salts, &c. fly away from the Body dissolved, leaving it foul and the Calx a dry Powder not easily flowing,"[97] as that is which has its Radical Humidity fixed with it.

8. We may observe in the Seeds of Vegetables, from their first Sprouting, they are supplied with the Radical Moisture which they draw, *viz.*, the Sap, which coalesces with it and so it proceeds to its ultimate Perfection, for that Rotation. But if the Seeds be moved by farther Rotations, they are again multiplied by the same Radical Moisture without end, as it were.

9. These things sufficiently prove to me, that no Liquor, though never so wonderfully drawn out of Salts, ever did, or ever will dissolve *Sol* Radically in the way of Generation.

10. B. What have you to object against our Matter being the right, since as I told you it was created of God, and contains in its Bowels all Metals, Mercury and Precious Stones.

11. *Investigator.* This is a pleasing Conceit, and may make a pretty Jingle in the Ears of very Ignorant Men. For though it is true that this Globe of Earth was created, and contains all these things in it, and as you said before produces them too, and though some Muds and Particular Earths will yield such Appearances in Distillation, as you have spoken of, what is this to the End you propose, *viz.*, the Perfect Tincture for Metals?

12. It is as obvious as the Sun at Noon-Day, that the *Terra Adamica, Terra Lemnia,* and *Terra Foliata,* spoken of by *Philosophers*, are vastly different and remote from any part that can be selected from this *Globe of Earth*, even though it should be such as was immediately contiguous to Gold, Silver or Mercury in the Mines, but is an Earth made by them, and which they often call their *Chaos*, out of which they can draw a Mercury of Super Eminent Virtues, as well as Perfect Gold

and Silver. Therefore must declare your Earth and Process to be but a Counterfeit, in my Opinion, fit to pass only amongst the most Ignorant. One of the Philosophers, speaking of their Earth, makes it to be the Blessing of *Joseph* (who was separated from his Brethren, as the Philosophers in this Art are) *Deut.* 33, which he renders thus:— "Blessed of the Lord be his Land, for the Apples of Heaven, for the Dew and for the Deep that lieth Beneath; for the Apples of Fruit both of Sun and Moon, for the top of the Ancient Mountains, for the Apples (or Sweetness) of the Everlasting Hills," &c. "Pray the Lord, my Son, from the Bottom of thy Heart, that he would bestow upon thee a Portion of this Blessed Land or Earth."

13. Another of them says, "Our Earth is not the Simple Element of Earth, but Elemental Earth, which has all the Elements proportionally mixed."[98] and in a degree reconciled, though not yet wholly purified nor fixed, and yet contain *Sol, Luna* and *Mercury* in its Bowels.

14. C. What have you against the Matter of Fact, which I related in the Process upon *Vitriol*, which the Gentlemen assured me, was told him as a certain Truth, by a Friend of his?

15. *Investigator.* For my own part, I take *Vitriol* to be effectually included under Salts, Alloms, &c. and in my Enquiry shall make it of no other account, whatever Opinion you may retain of it by virtue of the Hearsay assurance you mention; but since you do not seem satisfied, with what has been said, as sufficient to exclude it, I can but deliver it over to the Philosophers, and for Brevity, to Candid *Ripley* only:—

> "And be thou wise in choosing of thy Water,
> Meddle with no Salt, Sulphur, nor mean Mineral,
> For whatsoever anyone to thee do clatter, *i.e., Babble.*
> Our Sulphur and Mercury be only in Metals,
> Which Oils and Waters some Men call,
> Fowls and Birds with other Names many one,
> Because that Fools should never find our Stone."[99]

16. D. What we offered at our last Conference, comes very near the Intention of Philosophers, that is the Multiplication of Light; for, as we then said, we can produce out of a Dark Subject a Star, and we are persuaded, as this is a degree of Light, not to be contemned, it may, by Art, be multiplied.

17. *Investigator.* I told you my Opinion then, that the Multiplication of Light in a proper Subject was the ultimate Perfection of this Art. We are assured by the Philosophers, that it may be so multiplied, as to become permanent and never fading, as they witness. And as this is the top of this Art, so we find it is the Perfection of Divinity also. For as the Philosophers lead us from their *Chaos*, through various Operations to the Perfection of their Lights, so we are led by all the inspired Men, from the first *Chaos* of the World, through the many Dispensations of it, to the Perfection of Light, the *Heavenly Jerusalem*, which has no need of the Light of the Sun by Day, nor of the Moon, for there is no Night there. And so we see Fire is multiplied upon a proper Subject, and as *Norton* says, if a whole Shire were Flax, one Spark of Fire is capable of making the while so. But both Light and Fire must have its proper Subject, or they cannot be multiplied. We see that immense, as one may call it, Body of Light, this Sun, illuminates the proper Subject the Air, not Earth, &c. and how wonderfully is this done every Four and Twenty Hours, the whole Firmament being at length, from the first glimmering or least degree of Light, filled with its Ray; the Dimensions of it not to be computed. The thing therefore to be considered in the Philosophic Work, is the proper Subject of both giving and receiving Light; which I conceive is sufficiently hinted in the course of this Enquiry.

18. I know many have mightily boasted of a Star they could produce, as you say, from a Dark Subject, which, so far as has fallen under my Observation, has proven to them, whatever it might be in its own Nature, an *Ignis Fatuus*, and not a Pole or Star to steer by; and instead of guiding them in their course,

they have had many a weary Dance, persuading themselves all the while they were near their Journey's End, whereas they have found they had not been far from the place from whence they set out; and this they have repeated so often, it may be for many Years, till at length they Curse their *Astronomy*, and Swear there is no such Science. As though, because they cannot perform the desired Voyage by this Star, no Mariner could by any other of greater Altitude and Lucidity; but Experience teaches other ways. For Philosophers, steering chiefly by the *North Pole* and *Venus Orient*, can perform the Work; but by no others, if these are wanting. The latter, they say, is a Star of a Palish Purple Colour, showing its Solar Nature, and by whose means and assistance *Sol* himself arrives at the highest Colour and Tincture, which the Experienced know. The *Æsch Mezareph* fully showeth this, when he bids you not to be deceived by expecting *Nogah* (Venus), to be of a White Splendour, as the Word seemed to import; *but that it both has received and gives a Solar Nature*, as I have said, though itself is not yet mature and fixed.

19. You see now of what Nature and Consequence this Star is in their Astronomy and Navigation; such therefore as your Astronomy is, such will be your Navigation; if your Astronomy be good, you may pass, without fear, directly into the Ocean; if not, you must always remain in sight of Land, and never reach the Golden Coast.

20. It was by the Advice and Present of *Venus*, that *Hippomenes* overtook and enjoyed the Huntress, *Atalanta*. So Ripley advises to consult with *Venus* in the Beginning, as I hinted in the first Part. And as *Venus* furnished *Hippomenes* with Three Golden Apples, so did he as prudently use them; for after the first, she rather ran more nimbly than before, through the Joy of it; the second had a greater Effect, by taking up her Mind with the Beauty and Value of it; but the third, being seasonably applied, accomplishing the thing, and entirely stayed her being captivated with its Excellency.

21. Venture not therefore to run with *Atalanta*, without advising with *Venus*, lest you are slain instead of attaining her. Learn to know the use of this Star, I say, both Occidental and Oriental in your Voyage, or you may miserably rove and unawares run into a Gulf of Error.

22. To these we must add the Knowledge of their Magnet and Needle, which converts itself to the Pole, also the Points of their Compass, by which they Steer, then and not till then expect a Successful Voyage. If your Theory therefore be not right, it must be mended, and then your Practice will be soon so too, but not before: For otherwise should you put to Sea a Thousand times, it will be but as so many Casual Experiments, and Accidental Trials, which the Philosophers exclude from Success. Many things might be added concerning their Sea and Winds, and wherein they give Necessary Cautions about the contrary ones, but Experience will instruct when the Theory is complete.

23. D. You may remember our Opinion was, that the Fire of *Vulcan* was the Artificial Death of the Metals, &c.

24. *Investigator.* I will add the preceding and succeeding Words to those you urge, which to me seem a sufficient Answer to you. First, By showing that common Fire cannot destroy the Soul or Life of Gold and which is its Perfection: Secondly, That the Fire of *Vulcan* he speaks of, is not Culinary. "Gold Vulgar," says he, "is a Body, whose Soul is retired into a strong hold, that it may be defended from the Violence of the Fire. Therefore, saith the Philosophers, the Fire of *Vulcan* is the Artificial Death of Metals, and as many as have suffered Fusion, have in it lost their Life. If thou canst apply this wittily, both to thy imperfect Body and fiery Dragon, thou need no other Key to all our Secrets."[100] Make this witty Application, or you can reap no advantage; and as this is the Key to all their Secrets, so believe there are secret Wards in it.

25. To destroy Gold is not an easier task than to make it; to melt it in a Crucible is most easy, but the Fusion of it in the Fire of their *Vulcan* most secret. When Gold is melted in their Mercury, as Ice in warm Water, not only it's Soul but whole Form is taken from it. Nor are other Metals secure from the Force of this devouring Fire, nor is that any wonder when it can this overcome Gold itself, whose Perfection is such as to defend itself from the Violence of common Fire, though it cannot from the Power of this. If, when he says, "for our Gold is a *Chaos*, whose Soul is not put to flight by the Fire," he had added, "But Gold Vulgar is a Body, whose Soul is put to flight by the Fire, you might have had some Colour for your Inference;"[101] but he says just the contrary, that it neither is nor can be by common Fire, which, as I said before, is its Perfection. And which I think signifies plainly what he intended by thus expressing himself, *viz.*:– "Gold Vulgar is a Body of so great Strength, that it will be a hard Labour to draw his Soul from him; but our Gold is a *Chaos*, a tender Body, or rather a Spirit, whose Soul it retains in itself, as common Gold does, but contrary to that, this lies so open, that it is capable of suffering Hurt, and being put to flight by the Fire."[102]

26. In short, these as well as many other Places are part of that Subtle Stile I hinted in the Beginning, which contributes so much to the Impeding your Knowledge; for they know how to place their Words so as their Readers will be much more affected with the Shell of them, than discern the Kernel, *viz.*, their Intentions.

27. I own, many Philosophers have written of one Matter, which is "not perfected by Nature, nor wholly imperfect, but in the way to Perfection," as you before have said, and that this would perfect the Work of itself. But here we must again be careful of their Subtle way of Writing. For though I do believe they herein speak the Truth, (as I showed at out last Meeting concerning their *Chaos*, that it contained all things

requisite, as that of the *Chaos* of the World did, and which indeed is confirmed by the Universal Consent of Philosophers) yet in this also some necessary Cautions must be observed. For though they may say this Matter is produced by Nature, yet not by Nature alone, which makes a very wide difference. Nature may be said to make Man or a baby Chick, but not Nature alone without the help and will of Man concurring, and bringing Agent and Patient together; for unless Man take care to provide a Cock to tied the Hen, her Eggs will not produce a Chick. Hear *Sendivogius's* Opinion of this thing, who has most excellently determined the matter, *viz.*:— "I tell thee, my Son, one is not made of one Naturally; for this to do is proper to God alone: Let it suffice thee that thou art able out of two to make one, which will be profitable to thee."[103]

28. This is speaking of Multiplicative Generation, such as their Elixir, not of unary Perfections. For Nature doth produce Gold without the aid of Man, but as the Elixir is above the Power of Nature alone, so is the production of its First Matter. Though it must not be denied, but Nature furnishes the Materials, of which, by her Aid, Art makes the First Matter of the Stone to appear. And as the End is above the Power of Nature alone, so is the Beginning, and which I would advise you to take notice of. Therefore whatever Allusions, Metaphors or Ænigma's the Philosophers use, they assert, they must all be reduced to these standing Rules, some Exceptions to be allowed for Comparisons between Animal, Vegetable and Mineral Productions, which a discreet Artist will easily make. *Geber* says, "We find modern Artists describe to us but one only Stone, both for the White and Red, which we grant to be true, for in each Elixir there is no other thing than *Argent Vive* and Sulphur, therefore 'tis called by Philosophers one Stone, although 'tis drawn from divers things."[104] In another place he has, in a different way of Speaking, delivered is the Principles thus, "Our Stone is

no other than a Fœtent Spirit and Living Water, by a Natural Proportion, cleansed and united with such a union, that they cannot be separated from one another; this we call dry Water. To these two must be added also a third, for abbreviating the Work, namely a perfect Body attenuated."[105] As no Testimony can be clearer, so we need no Authority greater. Nor does he in the least contradict himself, when he says, "If you can complete it of *Argent Vive* alone, you will be the finder of a most precious Perfection."[106] Since even that is compounded of two, as is just above said, inseparably mixed and purified. For this *Argent Vive* has its own Volatile, pure Sulphur, and Arsenic in its Belly, which will congeal and fix it, and then it may be called *Sulphur*, which hide its own *Argent Vive* in its Belly, and defends it from the Violence of the Fire.

29. This Water thus united with its imperfect Body he calls, by way of Eminence, *Argent Vive of Argent Vive*, because it took its beginning "from the matter of *Argent Vive* which was created or natural,—Tho' not of its while Substance,"[107] for there are Superfluities thrown of, and a Spiritual Body introduced, and what is now visible, is part of the Created or Natural *Argent Vive*, and part of the Spiritual Body. And he puts this grand Question, as if it were on the behalf of Enquirers. "From what things this *Argent Vive* may be best extracted."[108]

30. And, in my Opinion, answers it as fully, *viz.*:— "It must be taken from those things in which it is; 'tis a well in Bodies, as in *Argent Vive* itself. Therefore of which ever sort the Medicine is, this precious Stone must be sought as well in Bodies as in the Substance of *Argent Vive*,—for it was never the Intention of Philosophers it should be sought elsewhere.—Our Ancestors could not, nor can we, nor shall they that come after us, find any other way, than by these things."[109]

31. This Experienced Philosopher leads us yet further to the Knowledge of the Principles, and by showing the Properties of the Medicine even draws a Consent, from the

careful Observers of it, that it can draw its Original from nothing else, according to the necessity of the Law of Nature. For if the Properties he mentions were duly considered, Sentence would pass at one upon most of the False and Foreign Matters. And indeed would help to regulate the Practice upon the True, for as he says, in the Preparation made by Sublimation, "Be not negligent, for such as its Preparation shall be, such will be its Perfection, some through negligence in Preparation, have made imperfect instead of perfect Bodies in Projection:—Have a care therefore thou dost not make Water of Death instead of Water of Life."[110]

32. This crafty Author has interspersed the greatest Truths amongst a Thousand Broileries and Subtle Inventions, which method he chose rather than Ænigmatical Discourses, as he owns, "But in such a way of speaking as is agreeable to the Will of the most High, Blessed, Sublime and Glorious God, who gives it to, and with holds it from whom he pleases."[111]

33. Thus has he under the known Names of *Argent Vive* and *Sulphur*, proposed the Generation of this most secret Stone, as others, especially the Ancient Poets, have done by abundance of Allegories, which taken other ways than Chymically, would not only be Monstrous but Impious, and, for the most part of them, without Foundation and Fabulous. However they concur in this, that Nature multiplies things by at least two Parents, God alone Creating from one, as has been said, and which ought not to be forgot. *Hermes* allows it not only a Father and Mother, but a Nurse: And *Lully* has not been wanting to assert that the Stone has two Fathers and two Mothers, alluding to its double Birth.

34. Others have assigned to their Offspring three Fathers, as in the Production of *Orion, i.e., Apollo, Vulcan* and *Mercury*; these are curious subtleties written and invented to amuse the Ignorant and hide the Art; however we may gather from these things Matter for every Purpose, and particularly I shall

observe to you one of their Allegories, upon occasion of your proposing to work in one thing alone.

35. They tell us that:— "Erichthonius sprung out of the Earth, whist *Vulcan* was Wrestling with *Pallas*, the reputed Goddess of Wisdom, and was Born without the Feet of a Man, *&c.* which is thus expounded. Such are those Persons, who by the means of *Vulcan* only, without the Wisdom of *Pallas*, do beget Offsprings that are Monstrous without Feet and abortive, which can neither profit others, nor benefit themselves. The two Legs are two Organic Members of Man, without which there can be not true walking; so likewise Medicine, and indeed every operative Art, are supposed to have two Legs.—But Chymistry in particular has two Subjects (as its Legs) of which one is the Key, the other a secure or fastened Lock, by which there will be a free admission into the Philosophers Rosary, to those who have a right to enter. But if one of these are wanting, it would be the same thing as if a Cripple should attempt to out-run a Hare. The Key is a thing of the meanest value, known in the Chapters, and is the Root and *Foundation of the Rosary*, or Garden of Roses, without which, not a Branch or Bud will put forth, or any Rose spring and send forth Leaves in a Thousand fold. It will Naturally be asked, where this Key is to be found or sought for? I answer with the *Oracle*, Where the Bones of Orestes were said to be found, *i.e.*, where THE WINDS, THE SMITER, THE RESISTER AND THE DESTRUCTION OF MEN are to be found together, *i.e.*, as *Lychas* expounds it, in a *Copper-Smith's* or Brasier's Work-house; for by the Winds, the Bellows; by the Smiter, the Hammer; by the Resister; the Anvil; and by the Destruction or Mischief of Men, Iron seems to have been meant by the Oracle. If a Man knows how to Number well, and distinguish the Signs, he will certainly find this Key in the Northern Hemisphere of the Zodiac, and the Lock in the Southern."[112]

36. (How Harmonious the Philosophers are we may see; if we duly observe, even in places least taken notice of. For *Æsch Mezareph* assigns the same places to this Lock and Key, *viz.:*—"Learn therefore to purify *Naaman* coming from the North, and acknowledge the Strength of *Jordan* flowing out of the North; but he that will" (thoroughly know or) "become wise, let him live in the South.") "And being Masters of these, it will be easy to open the door and enter, and in the very entrance he will see *Venus* with her beloved *Adonis*, for she has tinged the white Rose with a Purple Colour, with her blood."—Michael Maier.[113]

37. I shall be sorry any of you should be of that Number, mentioned by a Philosopher in *Turba Philosophorum, viz.*, be the worse for reading those things which are written for our Information, "Our Books prove very injurious to those who read them only once or twice, or perhaps thrice, whereas they are disappointed in the Understanding of them, and in their whole Study; and, which is worse, lose all their Money, Pains and Time, which they spend in this Art; and when a Man thinks he has the whole World he will find himself possest of nothing."[114] This is, as it often falls out, he has neither the Art, Money, nor Time left, and so expires in Ignorance, Sorrow and Poverty.

38. Many, says a Philosopher, are busy about washing *Latona*, when at the same time they know her not. Ripley says, many talk of *Robin-Hood* who never Shot in his Bow, therefore it seems they have sent us to the Work-house where she is wrought. Sometimes we are sent to the Potter, the Washer-Woman and the Cook. Sometimes to the Husband-Man, to the Hen and other Birds; then to the Fountains, Baths, Springs, Gardens, Rivers and Church yards. Sometimes to Geometry, Divinity and Music; then to the Sun, Moon and Stars. Sometimes to the Sea, Bottom of the Sea, Bowels of the Earth, and midst of the Air; to Man and Woman, and other

Animals; sometimes to the Mountains and Rocks, to the Four Elements and indeed to whole Nature. From hence, it is very easy for Men to please their several Fancies with this or the other matter, and give themselves a wonderful Entertainment in this Study, and yet unprofitably. For unless they make choice of the true, and knows it to be so, they remain Ignorant and Doubting, that is lame and deficient.

39. For when Knowledge is present, even but of their true matters, most if not every one of these things will be known, were they ten times as many; know the Work-house and the Tools mentioned, and know all, be ignorant of them, and ignorant of all their Allegories; another Specimen of which I shall recite from one of their best Expositors, *viz.*:– "Amongst the Philosophers they apply to their Sol the Names: Osiris, Dionysius, Bacchus, Jupiter, Mars, Adonis, Oedipus, Perseus, Achilles, Triptolemus, Hippomenes and Pollux. And their true Luna is: Isis, Juno, Venus, the Mother of Oedipus, Danae, Deidamia, Atalanta and Helena, as also Latona, Femele, Uropa, Leda, Antiope and Thalia; these are the parts of that Compound which before the Work is called the Stone, and by the Name of every Metal Magnesia: After Operation, Orcus, Pyrrhus, Apollo, Æsculapius. The adjuncts are, Typhon, Python, Aper; the Operators are denominated by Hercules, Ulysses, Jason, Theseus and Pirithous; and the dangers and labours which these underwent are innumerable."[115]

40. "We may see the Labours of Hercules; the Errors of Ulysses; the Dangers of Jason; the Endeavours of Theseus; and the Remoras of Pirithous. This is the great Matter and Doctrine" (of their Books) "through which in every Page Saturn, Mercury and Vulcan do often occur. The first as Father of all, without which nothing can be effected, the second as the Matter and Form, and the third as the Efficient. *Sol* takes *Luna* to be his Wife, *Jupiter* takes *Juno*, as *Saturn*, *Rheam*, and *Osiris*, *Isis*. *Dionysus* is snatched out of his Mother's Womb, who was

Burnt by the Thunder of *Jupiter*, that so be may be brought to Maturity in the Thigh of his Father *Jupiter, &c.*" And at last concludes, "And so you see there is a Concord in them all."– Michael Maier.[116] Make a right use of this Exposition, and you will be abundantly set to rights in your Enquiry.

41. Here we are told, this is the Matter and Doctrine of the Philosophers, and what does it contain? But a Duality of Matters; which is to my present purpose. Though these things may be varied many ways, besides showing the Power of Generation by two, which whole Nature bears witness to, and which is needless to show; it being too plain to admit of a dispute.

42. To keep therefore within the bounds mentioned, of *Saturn* and *Mercury*. *Saturn* as the Father of all, and *Mercury* the Matter and Form united, as you know *Saturn* himself, in Story, had two Parents. This Doctrine of *Saturn*, being the Father of all, agrees, again, exactly with *Æsch Mezareph*, in the place he gives their *Lead* or *Saturn*, which he calls *Chochmah*, and which he says, is the Father of all the following Natures, which come after it and perfect the Work. This *Lead* or *Saturn*, in another place he says is Mystically called Col (or Chol) which is, all; because therein lies the System of all Universality.

43. Again he describes this Matter thus, "The Metallic Root [here] possesses the Place of Kether, which hath a hidden Nature lying under great Obscurity, and from which all Metals have their Original; even as all the rest of the Sephiroth are hid in the Nature of *Kether*, and flow from thence."[117] *Saturn* you know is reputed to be the Discoverer of Truth, and another adds, if *Saturn* be really present you cannot Err. Don't be too confident, you know this *Saturn*, for here lies Wisdom, truly known to none but her Children, and not to the Vulgar, who can behold but externally, but are Ignorant of what it contains, but the Scholar of Wisdom goes on to analyse it, and then he will be made Rich as well as Wise.

44. Some I know take this matter to be the Mineral of Lead, others a Saturnine Mineral, more crude than that, or it may be, this commixt with a Metal, and yet not Maleable; but as it is allowable for an Enquirer to explain his own meaning, I do say that for my own part I have not been speaking of a matter so familiar to Enquirers, as may at first be imagined, but of an *Anomalous Subject*, of which indeed you often speak and read, but know not the Virtue and Beauty which is in it, for if you can make this *Saturn* Vomit up the Stone he has devoured, you will obtain your desire, the Power of doing which is given to *Mercury* and *Venus*, by whose Mediation, Interposition and Help, the Stone will be produced, but never the Red without the Purple Star of the latter.

45. These are called by *Æsch Mezareph*, "*Netzach* and *Hod* which are the places of the Body; and the Seminal Receptacles are referred to the place of Hermaphroditical Brass."[118] You know the Story makes *Mercury* and *Venus* the Parents of *Hermaphroditus*, which is Synonymous with *Rebis*, of which the Books of Philosophers ring, as also with *Androgynus*, who is feigned to have two Heads. But it must still be observed, *Hermaphroditus* sprung from two, as did *Saturn* himself. Therefore it thou knowest this matter, and esteemest it as thou ought, and canst cause it to put off its foul Garments, thou art blessed by God with no mean Talent.

46. Thus have the Philosophers pointed out this Secret Art under Veils and Allegories, not to prostitute it, no; God and Nature forbidding; it is a Science too excellent and admits of no compare, though there are many very useful ones, but this may rather be said, virtually, to contain them all, and is even the best Expositor of Divinity itself, not only by showing the Creation and Destruction of the World, but the true Figure of Mortification, Regeneration, Redemption and Exaltation, set before the Eyes of the Body, and which are in a most lively manner impressed upon the Soul; and the Mind is so furnished

with the Knowledge of a Trinity in Unity, as not to admit of a doubt concerning so Divine and Mysterious a Truth.

47. The Philosophers having so large a scope, no wonder their Books have been filled with such Various Similitudes, &c., and which have afforded so many Amusements to the Readers, that almost every one furnishes himself with a different Theory and Practice, and thereby clothes himself with an Opinion of his great Ability and Skill, when at the same time they are Ignorant of the things whereof the Philosophers speak, thinking if they knew but this or the other Riddle, they were Cock-sure of the Art.

48. Whereas if they had Twenty of them unfolded in the same Language, they would be as much to seek as before. As for Instance, that propounded by *Sphynx* to *Oedipus*. "What is that which in the Morning goes on four Feet, as Noon upon two, and in the Evening upon three?"[119] The Critics may very Naturally apply it to the Age of a Man, who at first is only able to crawl upon four, in his Middle State walk upon two, and in Old Age with a Staff upon three; but Chymically, which is its true intent, it is expounded thus, "A Quadrangle or Four Elements are first of all to be considered, from hence we come to the Hemisphere, having two lines, a right and a curve, that is to the White Luna, from thence to the Triangle, which consists of Body, Soul and Spirit, or Sol, Luna and Mercury. ... *The Stone*, says Rafis, is a Triangle in its Essence, a Quadrangle in its Qualities."[120]

49. And another adds, a Circle, in its invariable Redness. If many of the other Emblematical Figures mentioned by Philosophers, and with which so many are amused at this Day, were explained in the same manner, where would they be who place their greatest hopes in them? Whether would they fly to supply the want of them in their Study? Or how far would it profit them? I fear but little.

50. Things known and common are often despised, whilst things concealed, though not of equal value, are earnestly sought. "What is more useful than Fire and more precious than Water? What more amiable than the Earth clothed with Flowers and all things which are Beautiful? What more delightful than Air? Which when 'tis obstructed will make all things cease to seem pleasant! But in their vast Spheres they are exposed to the common use of Mankind, and, by a preposterous Imagination, they are thought to be of no value."[121]

51. Don't therefore be of that Number, who neglect and despise known things, and seek with all their might those which are Fabulous and at best but Metaphorical; spoken, not to lead but mislead you; these, whilst they remain Riddles, mightily amuse, and when unfolded their Virtues ceases. Such things serve to show the Wit of the Inventor, more than the Value of the things themselves. For if by such a Wit, the Skill and Practice of the Husband-man were drawn into fine-spun Riddles, how great would be the Amusement? How high might the Expectation be raised, but with what Profit? And even when unfolded, it would result in this, *viz.*, it is very true, and these things we daily see before our Eyes. As there is a great deal of Danger attends, and many Mischiefs ensue an eager pursuit of Shadows, neglecting the plain course of Nature, so I would Caution against it, as Impediments rather than Helps.

52. For Fables, nay even Miracles themselves, are more easily Misunderstood than Comprehended, unless by the Authors of them.

53. E. You have not spoken anything to what I proposed, Pray let me hear what you have to say concerning the Particular I mentioned at our last Conference.

54. *Investigator.* As it does not concern this Enquiry, which is about the secret Philosophy of the *Hermetic Art*, I shall only leave with you an Established Authority, and not trouble you with mine, which I know you would dispute. *Sendivogius* writes to

this Effect, *viz*.:– "There is, as we have said, but one Operation, and beside it there is no other that is true; all they therefore are mistaken, that say, that any particular thing besides this one way and natural matter, is true; for a Bough is not to be had but from the Trunk of a Tree: It is an impossible and senseless thing to go about to produce a Bough; it is easier to make the Elixir itself, than any particular thing, although most simple, that will be Profitable, and abide a Natural Examination and Trial.–But seeing there are as many Opinions as Men, we will leave everyone to his own Opinion: Let him that will not follow our Counsel and imitate Nature remain in his Error. Indeed particulars may easily be made, if you have a Tree, whose Young Twigs may be grafted into divers Trees.–There be many Artificers who seek their own Fancies: They seek a new Nature and a new Matter, and in conclusion find a new Nothing, because they interpret the Writings of Philosophers, not according to the Possibility of Nature, but the Letter."[122]

55. I have trespassed upon your Patience, Gentlemen, and could very largely proceed, but a great many Words was never my design any more than they would be your Profit, therefore have comprised this my Enquiry in as few as I could conveniently contrive. And though I have not whetted your expectations by great assurances of my Ability, not the Title of *Master*, I hope it will not, as I am sure it ought not, lessen what is said.

56. I write not for your applause, nor seek your approbation no farther than it may be to your own advantage; but give me leave to say, I never had troubled myself nor you, unless I had entertained an Opinion that some of the more judicious would reap a Benefit from so candid a Relation of what an Enquirer had observed and knows to be truly stated. And for the sake of such suffer me to add, without going out of my Province, that these are not random Guesses, nor undigested Speculations, but such as will find a place in all Ages to come, amongst the

Knowing in this Science, or this Enquiry had never seen the Light. Therefore I shall conclude, with this Advice, take *Nature* for your Guide, the *Philosophers* for your Counsellors, *Reason* and *Experience* for your Assistants, and Lay your Foundation Deep and Wide even as Wide as whole Nature; don't let it be Shallow nor Narrow, if it be, it will not support the Work.

57. Let there be chosen a sure Foundation Stone, squared according to God's Command and Law, *Genesis*, i. 11, "And God said, let the Earth bring forth Grass yielding Seed and the Fruit Tree yielding Fruit after its kind, whose Seed is in itself, *&c.,*" and it was so, and remains so to this Day. Our Blessed Redeemer says, that if the Seed remains alone, it will not Germinate, nor Increase unless it die, and then it will rise again and multiply. The philosophers unanimously concur, that Gold has likewise its Seed in itself, which, they also teach, must die, that is put off its Form and then it rises again Gloriously to Multiplication.

58. You are not Ignorant that what I say is undeniably and constantly maintained by them. Therefore for what end should I enlarge to Elucidate these things? If what is said will not affect your Study and Practice, more will not. If you will not be instructed by God and Christ, Nature and the Philosophers, how can I expect you will be more attentive to what I say? Though I will add, to heighten your attention, Nature, by her Daily Actions before your Eyes, sufficiently confirms these things, in the Multiplication of the several Species.

NOTES

"HERMETIC ART."

---

1. *Hermetic;* alluding to Hermes Trismegistus: a mythical Magus who has given his name to many treatises on western Occultism and Alchemy. The names of Hiram King of Tyre, Chiram Abif and Hermes have been counter changed; and the Kabbalistic Key applied to the name throws some light on the actual meaning of the Alchemical process,—taking the Hebrew lettering Ch I R M, we get the falling dew containing that principle of life reproduction—Nitrogen, working in darkness upon the perfectible body. Also an expert may here discern an allusion to the wonderful power of chlorine on Gold. The merest tyro in chemistry knows the famous *Aqua Regia* of the ancients was a cunningly manufactured liquor bearing a close resemblance to the fluid obtained by the mixture of Nitric acid and Hydrochloric acid.—S.S.D.D.

2. *Art.*—The Hermetic Science being the Ethical side of Western Occultism; the Hermetic art may be regarded as the practical application of the same on all planes, from those of pure reason and exalted consciousness through those of human life down to the most material; from the regeneration and purification of the soul, to the regeneration and purification of the baser metals.—S.S.D.D.

3. *To the perfection of Sol and Luna.*—These words are much in favour with masters of the mysteries who are desirous of hiding their meaning. They are used in a hundred different ways, signifying active and passive; male and female; sudden rapid vibration, and solid resisting substance; gold, and silver; red rust of iron;

blue vitriol, *i.e.,* sulphate of copper, green sulphate of iron, and sulphide of antimony. Throughout the Alchemic processes they have been used to denote the force and the substance; the transmitter and the transmuted. And wise is he whose solar power has the penetrating force to discern the truth in the lunar shades with which he is surrounded.–S.S.D.D.

4. *Have Justified one another's testimony.*–Here we have a ray of hope, for those who have read many alchemical treatises will find that there are startling agreements in the teachings of some of the best works, such as those of Clavius, Rosenstein, Becker, Ponia and others who give more practical directions than vague writers like Geber, Bacon and Flamel.–S.S.D.D.

5. *The Art altogether impossible.*–The position taken up is natural enough. No man could with reasonable hope of success, hope to transform a fully grown elm tree into an oak, just as impossible would it seem to transmute a lump of copper into a lump of gold. But the Alchemists did not assert this to be possible, until both metals were reduced to one original basic substance, which they call Hylē and which we call Protyle in the mineral, or Protoplasm in the animal world. It was under these circumstances that they asserted transmutation to be possible; and it is in this relation we find the deep significance of the mystical death and resurrections of Osiris, Buddha and Christ. "Unless ye be born again ye cannot enter into the kingdom of perfection;» Unless the imperfect metal is destroyed, it cannot rise again into perfection. See also Eugenius Philalethes in his tract called *Euphrates or the Waters of the East,* printed in 1655.–S.S.D.D.

6. An anonymous Alchemic Essay, written in the time of Queen Elizabeth, published by Elias Ashmole, 1658; this famous antiquary also issued Alchemic books under the title of *"James Hasolle, Qui est Mercuriophilus Anglicus."*–S.S.D.D.

7. Author of *Crede Mihi* or *The Ordinall of Alchymy,* written about 1477.–S.S.D.D.

8. *The chief impediments.*–Three out of a million men, says Norton, may be ordained for Alchemy. Now some light may be thrown on the true Nature of the Art by this statement. It is no common gift that is needed, and without delay of argument I may safely

assert that the proportions mentioned points at once to the fact that only persons of genius can hope to attain the perfection of this Art of Arts. It is the Art of living in the divine light; the Art of knowing, the Art of "being one" with the highest universal consciousness. No talent will give insight to the man who is unable to bring about this regeneration of his soul; no labour will avail him who has shut out the life of the universe from his little life. The man of genius, the divine artificer of his soul must make himself, and know himself to be, one with the least of created things, and then and then only will he know what it is to be one with the Creator.–S.S.D.D.

9. See, *The Hermetic Arcanum* of Espagnet, paragraph 4.–S.S.D.D.

10. The Adept, like the poet, is born not made.–S.S.D.D.

11. Geber, the Arab alchemist, died about 740 A.D., his real name was *Abu Musa Jafar al Sofi.*–S.S.D.D.

12. Michael Sendivogius lived about 1636, was the editor of the *Dialogue between Mercury, Nature and the Alchemist,* and other works designed if not completed by his Master, Alexander Seton.–S.S.D.D.

13. *This mysterious way of writing.*–*For* the guidance of those who propose to study ancient and mediæval writers on Alchemy, I may say that the work naturally divides itself into three parts; and each of these into three processes, decoction, distillation, cohobation. The first part is the preparation of the Body or matter; the second is preparation of the soul or medium; and the third is preparation of the spirit or active principle. Take the three principles of the Alchemists, being the time honoured veils under which truth has been hid. Call the body–sulphur, the soul–salt, and the spirit–mercury. Purify each separately, then must these three become one; they must rise; they must fall; they must circulate in the vessel. And this is the fourth work. This is simple enough and is the mere ordinary process of subliming with heat, cohobating the separated parts, and subliming again until the body becomes spiritual, the spirit become corporified, the impure becomes pure, and nothing is wasted, but all is found in its right place, and the perfection or right proportion is attained.–S.S.D.D.

14. Lived about 1160, A.D.; he wrote two works, *On the Philosopher's Stone* and *The Art of Prolonging Life:* they were published in Paris in 1657.—S.S.D.D.

15. *Take one thing.*—Just as on the human plane you take the one man; and reduce him in thought down to the cell unit, so the alchemists reduced their one substance to its simplest form, and found things all latent therein.—S.S.D.D.

16. Ariadne, daughter of Minos, King of Crete, furnished to Theseus a thread by which to pass through the Labyrinth, and so reach the Minotaur, for the purpose of slaying it.—S.S.D.D.

17. That is, as soon as anyone develops his power of intuition, of reading between the lines, and of understanding the oriental passion of allegory that permeates mystical and religious writers, the meaning of many statements, utterly absurd if interpreted literally, will appear plain to the enlightened mind.—S.S.D.D.

18. *Diana.*—The moon goddess, answering to what has of late been called the astral body or aura; the sensitive radiations of which convey impressions to our bodily sense organs. *The Fountain* alludes to the universal source of life and light with which it is the object of the occult student to bring his astral life into touch.—S.S.D.D.

19. *The Secret Way of Philosophers.*—The philosophers know well enough that the first study for mankind is Man; to know thyself is to know nature. To become an adept of power is to possess the key of all the secrets of nature because you possess the key to your own nature.—S.S.D.D.

20. The above explains why in *this* work we do *not* begin with Quicksilver.—S.S.D.D.

21. By Eirenæus Philalethes, whose name is unknown; *The Open Entrance to the Shut Palace of the King,* first published at Amsterdam, 1668; a masterly work of very great interest.—W.W.W.

22. This is the first practical remark, on the subject of metals, in the treatise. It may here be noted that common quicksilver dissolves into a liquid resembling water in appearance if mixed with a proportion of one to ten of nitric acid.—S.S.D.D.

23. *The perfect body.*–Gold undergoes a considerable change when mixed with Mercury. The imperfect body Mercury can be reduced to subtle Water with nitric acid.–S.S.D.D.

24. See, Bernard of Treves: the Fountain was a symbol specially used by him.–S.S.D.D.

25. Very well describes the ordinary corrosive sublimate of commerce.–S.S.D.D.

26. It may here be noted that the sign of Mercury combines the lunar and solar symbols.–S.S.D.D.

27. Jean d'Espagnet: see Volume I of the *Collectanea Hermetica.*–S.S.D.D.

28. Compare the *Emerald Tablet* of Hermes Trismegistus.–S.S.D.D.

29. Arnold of Villanova, born 1245, a physician, a professor at the University of Barcelona.–S.S.D.D.

30. *Moist fire* describes nothing in nature more accurately than the liquid acids of commerce; but let the student be warned that many authors expressly deny that this is the real meaning of the term.–S.S.D.D.

31. Sentences in fancy brackets "{ }" were in the original *A short Enquiry Concerning the Hermetick Art*, 1714 edition, and not in the Westcott 1894 edition.–D.K.

32. See what is said previously of the words *Sol* and *Luna*, Note 3.–S.S.D.D.

33. Magnesia, is the oxide of the metal Magnesium, in modern chemistry; this is not what is referred to.–S.S.D.D.

34. Litharge, is an impure oxide of lead; this is not here intended.–S.S.D.D.

35. There is an elaborate treatise called "The Privy Seal of Secrets, which upon pain of damnation is not unadvisedly to be broken up nor revealed to any but with great care and many cautions." Circa 1680, in which it is asserted that "the first matter of the philosophers is a glutinous or clayey substance."–S.S.D.D.

36. Sir George Ripley, Canon of Bridlington, lived about 1490.–S.S.D.D.

37. *The Green Lion.*–I here reprint an ancient receipt for the manufacture of this mystic animal, or of his prototype:–

80

℞. Sea salt; purify by dissolving it in dew; expose it to the beams of the Moon, uncovered in a wide basin; cover it with a glass cover and leave it in the rays of the Sun; this repeat during forty nights and days. Put it into a large high glass body; imbibe gradually with very strong and clear distilled vinegar, until it is thoroughly diluted, close it, and set it to putrefy for two or three days in a gentle heat. Distil this per alembic in a sand bath, and the spirit of the vinegar will come over; when the Green Oil comes, change the receiver quickly. Pour back the distilled vinegar and leave it to putrefy, you will then obtain more Green Oil by again distilling.–S.S.D.D.

38. Name of author unknown. This is a short essay which has been attributed to Lully or his friend Cremer of Westminster.–S.S.D.D.

39. Raymond Lully, a Spanish priest, died in 1314, on the coast of Africa, being stoned to death by Mohammedans.–S.S.D.D.

40. "To make *Sphæra Saturni Paracelsi*. Take salt-petre, 2 ounces; potass. carb. 1 ounce; Reg. Aut. Mast 4½ ounces; tartar in crystals, 1 ounce: common salt half an ounce; pulverise separately and mix together. Put the whole into a large crucible and let it melt gently in a wind furnace. Stir with a red hot tobacco pipe and unite ingredients well, pour into an iron cone and you will find your treasure at the bottom."–S.S.D.D.

41. Jean d'Espagnet, see paragraph 15 of the *Hermetic Arcanum*.–S.S.D.D.

42. See paragraph 52 of the *Hermetic Arcanum*.–S.S.D.D.

43. *Novum Lumen Chymicum,* by Seton and Sendivogius.–S.S.D.D.

44. Bacon, lived about 1270.–S.S.D.D.

45. Raymond Lully.–S.S.D.D.

46. Westcott changed the sentence from what was printed in the 1714 edition which read as follows, "the Philosophers have left in their Books."–D.K.

47. A Greek philosopher of the Ionic School, born 500 B.C.–S.S.D.D.

48. Compare, "I come not to send peace, but a sword."–S.S.D.D.

49. "The Gods made blind (or mad) him whom they doom to destruction." The Latin being: "Quem Deus vult perdere prius dementat."–S.S.D.D.

50. The 1714 edition used "green grass" and the Westcott edition used "green leaves." I have choose to use the 1714 edition.–D.K.

51. The 1714 edition used "extraordinary Value" and the Westcott edition used "extraordinary esteem." I have choose to use the Westcott edition.–D.K.

52. There is a portion of the Royal Arch Ceremony of Freemasonry which seems related to this symbolism.–S.A.

53. A delightful example of mystification.–N.O.M.

54. *Dove* in Hebrew is I U N H, pronounced Yoneh, and by Gematria = 10+6+50+5 = 71 = 8; this multiplied by 2 (the 2 Doves) = 16 which again can be reduced to 7, the number of Venus. Doves also being birds signify the sublimed metal, that is the part which flies upwards under the influence of heat.–S.S.D.D.

55. *Luna* in Hebrew I R Ch, pronounced Yaraich.–S.S.D.D.

56. Isaiah xxx. 26. "Moreover the light of the moon shall be as the light of the sun, *etc.*"–S.S.D.D.

57. "My dove my undefiled is but one."–S.S.D.D.

58. The four wings of two birds; taking this Leopard to be Mercury in its aspects of Corrosive Sublimate, which a century or two back was made by dissolving quicksilver in *Aqua fortis, i.e.,* nitric acid, and uniting it with sea salt, containing hydrochloric acid; it is possible to understand the two birds as signifying nitrogen and chlorine gas, which with heat would doubtless "exasperate the beast."–S.S.D.D.

59. The original of these scattered quotations will be found in the Latin *Kabbalah Denudata* of Knorr von Rosenroth, the *Æsch Mezareph* of which is to be republished in this series. This Alchemical portion of the work, the *Æsch Mezareph or Refining Fire,* is given by Eliphaz Levi in the *Clef des Grands Mystères* in disjointed paragraphs, and he asserts it to be the book of *Abraham the Jew,* which revealed so much to Nicholas Flamel, and he exemplifies his explanations of its *inner* meaning with Flamel's well-known plates.–S.S.D.D.

60. *The Mercury of the Philosophers,* Now though the Alchemists did use Mercury, as is proved by Norton's list of materials, yet one thing is asserted by them over and over again, and that is, that the "Mercury of the Philosophers" is not Quicksilver. The passage alluded to, in the *Æsch Mezareph,* but not quoted, as the "Treatise on Sulphur," is as follows: "For that sulphur of gold and iron whose extraction is taught by many and is easy; also of gold, iron, and copper, also of gold, iron, copper, and antimony, which are gathered together by vinegar after fulmination out of the lixivium, being changed into a Red Oil with a moist Hydrargyrum do tinge silver."–S.S.D.D.

61. Query, hindrance.–S.S.D.D.

62. To be reprinted in a future volume of this series.–S.S.D.D.

63. The words alluded to by Pontanus are in the third chapter of the *Secret Book of Artephius.* "Antimonium est de partibus Saturni, et in omnibus modis habet naturam ejus. Antimonium Saturni, convenit Soli." See Salmon's edition. ["Antimony is a mineral participating of Saturnine parts, and has in all respects the nature thereof. This Saturnine Antimony agrees with Sol."]–S.S.D.D.

64. Sendivogius.–S.S.D.D.

65. Compare Note 13.–S.S.D.D.

66. The 1714 edition used "foul Minera" and the Westcott edition used "fond Minera." I have choose to use the 1714 edition.–D.K.

67. Our author finishes up with a poem which a learned friend of mine would call "As clear as mud." However, I will make an effort to throw light upon some of the riddles it propounds. We have seen the *Green Lion* may be taken to mean a certain corrosive fluid concocted from sea salt and other ingredients, this must be mixed with the Martial Cadmus and the medicine of purification or Diana. In this mixture sea salt must be used, because it contains the universal Lunar Mercury or first Ens of Mercury. Ferrous sulphate or cuprous sulphate should be added to introduce the mercury of copper or iron into the resulting sublimate, indicated by the wings alluded to in the text. The whole alludes to the making of Sal Alembroth, which contains the secret fire and stirs up matter to action.–S.S.D.D.

68. The 1714 edition misspelled the word "entertain'd" instead using "entain'd". There was a hand-written note correcting the spelling mistake in the 1714 edition at the British Library. The Westcott edition used the word "enchain'd." I have decided to use the hand-written correction.—D.K.

69. The New Uprising Sun of course alludes to the material work of gold-making, and the author finishes up by a commendation of the happier state of those who find Rest in God alone. In this connection I may quote from the *Suggestive Enquiry*, printed half a century ago:— "What imagination is strong or hardy enough to glance into the full faith? *To be* the understanding of that Light of which all nature is the efflux. *To move* one with the First Mover and *be* his will.—Increase thyself into an immeasurable greatness, leaping beyond all bodies, and transcending time, become Eternity, and thou shalt understand God. If thou canst become higher than all height, lower than all depth, thou shalt comprehend in thyself the qualities of all creatures. Conceive likewise that thou canst at once be everywhere. Learn to know thyself, not yet begotten, young, old, dead, the things after death and all of these together, else thou canst not yet understand God. But if thou hast shut up thy soul, blinding it, fettering it, saying I understand nothing, I can do nothing. I am afraid of the sea; I cannot climb up into Heaven; I know not who I am; I cannot tell what I shall be; What hast thou to do with God? It is the greatest evil not to know that there is a God-power latent in man."

By the "I AM" is signified, in the *Kabbalah*, the subjective unity of all; the affirmation that there is one Fountain from which all nature flows. The knowledge of this Identity with nature in its first substance is the source of miracles due to the magical accords of colours, numbers, harmonies and planetary circulations, and all manifestation of vibration. The visible springs from the Invisible. "Human power is limited only by the poverty of its Imagination and the pettiness of its Will."—S.S.D.D.

70. *The Short Enquiry Concerning the Hermetic Art*, Part II is reprinted from the London, 1715 edition.—D.K.

71. This was quoted from *A New Light of Alchymie* by Michael Sendivogius. Translated out of the Latin into English by J[ohn] F[rench]. London: Printed by Richard Cotes, for Thomas Williams, 1650.–D.K.

72. Quoted from "The Fountain of Chemical Truth or Philosophy" in *Three Tracts of the Great Medicine of Philosophers for humane and metalline bodies.* All written in Latin by Eirenæus Philalethes. Translated into English for the benefit of the studious, by a lover of art and them. London: Printed and sold by T. Sowle, at the Crooked-Billet in Holy-well-Lane Shoreditch, 1694.–D.K.

73. *A New Light of Alchymie* by Michael Sendivogius, 1650.–D.K.

74. *A New Light of Alchymie* by Michael Sendivogius, 1650.–D.K.

75. This and the previous verse were quoted from "Upon the Elixir" by Pearce the Black Monk in *Theatrum Chemicum Britannicum.* Edited by Elias Ashmole, 1652.–D.K.

76. Quoted from "Anonymi, or several Works of unknown Authors" in *Theatrum Chemicum Britannicum.* Edited by Elias Ashmole, 1652.–D.K.

77. Quoted from "A Short Worke That beareth the Name ... of George Ripley" in *Theatrum Chemicum Britannicum.* Edited by Elias Ashmole, 1652.–D.K.

78. "Upon the Elixir" by Pearce the Black Monk, 1652.–D.K.

79. This quote is from [*Secrets Reveal'd: or,*] *An Open Entrance to the Closed Palace of the King* by Eirenæus Philalethes. English translation. London, 1669. It was published in Latin as *Introitus Apertus ad Occlusum Regis Palatium* in Amsterdam, 1668.–D.K.

80. Quoted from *The Mirror of Alchimy* by Roger Bacon. London, 1597.–D.K.

81. [*Secrets Reveal'd: or,*] *An Open Entrance to the Closed Palace of the King* by Eirenæus Philalethes. London, 1669.–D.K.

82. This was quoted from "Compound of Alchemy" (also known as the *Twelve Gates*) by Sir George Ripley in *Theatrum Chemicum Britannicum.* Edited by Elias Ashmole, 1652.–D.K.

83. Quoted from *The Short Enquiry Concerning The Hermetic Art.* London, 1714.–D.K.

85

84. This quote is from *Ripley Revived* by Eirenæus Philalethes. London: Printed for William Cooper at the Pellican on Little Britain, 1677.–D.K.

85. This was quoted from *The Hermetic Arcanum* by Jean d'Espagnet. Paris, 1623.–D.K.

86. *The Hermetic Arcanum* by Jean d'Espagnet. Paris, 1623.–D.K.

87. *The Hermetic Arcanum* by Jean d'Espagnet. Paris, 1623.–D.K.

88. *A New Light of Alchymie* by Michael Sendivogius, 1650.–D.K.

89. This quote is from "The Ordinall of Alchymie" by Thomas Norton in *Theatrum Chemicum Britannicum*. Edited by Elias Ashmole, 1652.–D.K.

90. "The Ordinall of Alchymie" by Thomas Norton, 1652.–D.K.

91. *The Hermetic Arcanum* by Jean d'Espagnet. Paris, 1623.–D.K.

92. "The Ordinall of Alchymie" by Thomas Norton, 1652.–D.K.

93. "The Ordinall of Alchymie" by Thomas Norton, 1652.–D.K.

94. "The Ordinall of Alchymie" by Thomas Norton, 1652.–D.K.

95. *The Short Enquiry Concerning the Hermetic Art*, Part III is reprinted from the London, 1715 edition.–D.K.

96. This was quoted from *The Works of Geber*. His real name was *Abu Musa Jafar al Sofi*. Faithfully Englished by Richard Russel. London: Printed for N.E. by Thomas James, and are to be sold by Robert Clavel, 1678.–D.K.

97. "Compound of Alchemy" by Sir George Ripley, 1652.–D.K.

98. [*Secrets Reveal'd: or,*] *An Open Entrance to the Closed Palace of the King* by Eirenæus Philalethes. London, 1669.–D.K.

99. "Compound of Alchemy" by Sir George Ripley, 1652.–D.K.

100. [*Secrets Reveal'd: or,*] *An Open Entrance to the Closed Palace of the King* by Eirenæus Philalethes. London, 1669.–D.K.

101. [*Secrets Reveal'd: or,*] *An Open Entrance to the Closed Palace of the King* by Eirenæus Philalethes. London, 1669.–D.K.

102. [*Secrets Reveal'd: or,*] *An Open Entrance to the Closed Palace of the King* by Eirenæus Philalethes. London, 1669.–D.K.

103. *A New Light of Alchymie* by Michael Sendivogius, 1650.–D.K.

104. *The Works of Geber*. Geber (*Abu Musa Jafar al Sofi*), 1678.–D.K.

105. *The Works of Geber*. Geber (*Abu Musa Jafar al Sofi*), 1678.–D.K.

106. *The Works of Geber*. Geber (*Abu Musa Jafar al Sofi*), 1678.–D.K.

107. *The Works of Geber*. Geber (*Abu Musa Jafar al Sofi*), 1678.–D.K.

108. *The Works of Geber.* Geber (*Abu Musa Jafar al Sofi*), 1678.–D.K.

109. *The Works of Geber.* Geber (*Abu Musa Jafar al Sofi*), 1678.–D.K.

110. This quote is from *Atalanta Fugiens: An Edition of the Emblems* by Michael Maier. Latin edition. Oppenheim publisher, Johann Theodor de Bry, 1618.–D.K.

111. *Atalanta Fugiens: An Edition of the Emblems* by Maier, 1618.–D.K.

112. *Atalanta Fugiens: An Edition of the Emblems* by Maier, 1618.–D.K.

113. *Atalanta Fugiens: An Edition of the Emblems* by Maier, 1618.–D.K.

114. This quote is from *Turba Philosophorum* by Guglielmo Gratarolo. Basel, 1613.–D.K.

115. *Atalanta Fugiens: An Edition of the Emblems* by Maier, 1618.–D.K.

116. *Atalanta Fugiens: An Edition of the Emblems* by Maier, 1618.–D.K.

117. Quoted from *Æsch Mezareph* which was printed along with *A Short Enquiry Concerning the Hermetic Art.* London, 1714.–D.K.

118. *Æsch Mezareph* which was printed along with *A Short Enquiry Concerning the Hermetic Art.* London, 1714.–D.K.

119. *Atalanta Fugiens: An Edition of the Emblems* by Maier, 1618.–D.K.

120. *Atalanta Fugiens: An Edition of the Emblems* by Maier, 1618.–D.K.

121. *Atalanta Fugiens: An Edition of the Emblems* by Maier, 1618.–D.K.

122. *A New Light of Alchymie* by Michael Sendivogius, 1650.–D.K.

Exterior of the Athanor invented by Geber.
Summa Perfectionis Magisterij. London, (1542).

APPENDIX I:

Review - The Hermetic Art, Vol. III *Collectanea Hermetica* edited by Dr Wynn Westcott.[1]

THE HERMETIC ART is Vol. III of *Collectanea Hermetica* edited by Dr. Wynn Westcott, and has a preface by "Non Omnis Moriar" and an Introduction and Notes by "S.S.D.D." Most of the text consists of warnings of the difficulty in understanding the subject and of the few who ever do, and one passage shows how the Philosophers "take the liberty" of contradicting themselves and each other. Still, this is not to be used as an argument against them or their Art, or even against the propriety of publishing further unintelligible works; rather is it a "trial of faith", as good Christians would express it. And all the difficulties vanish when one once gets the key—if one ever does. One can possess himself of some of these difficulties (though without the key) by investing $1.00 in this little work of fifty-two pages, wherein, partly in multi-capitalled prose and partly in what passed for poetry in a less exacting age, he can read about "Hunting the Green Lion", "The Doves of Diana", "Leprous Gold", "Metallic Moisture", and other profound mysteries understood only by the elect. (Orderable from PATH).—A[lexander] F[ullerton].

Notes:
1. "Review - The Hermetic Art, Vol. III *Collectanea Hermetica* edited by Dr Wynn Westcott" by A[lexander] F[ullerton] is reprinted from *The Path*, Vol. 9; No. 4, New York, July, 1894, p. 132.—D.K.

APPENDIX II:

A SHORT ENQUIRY CONCERNING THE HERMETIC ART.[1]

Most cordially do we welcome this third volume of *The Collectanea Hermetica,* which Dr. Westcott is reproducing. These volumes will do much to convince students of Occultism that they cannot afford to neglect the writings of Western Mystics. Those to whom the Alchymical symbology and style are more comprehensible than those of the Eastern systems will find here a valuable aid. In the preface we are informed that *The Short Enquiry* was first published in 1714,[2] and is written with especial reference to a work called The *Æsch Mezareph,* which connects physical Alchymy with the Kabbalah. The author, whose treatise is aptly summarized in the preface, argues for the truth of Alchymy on the ground of the universal agreement, as to essentials, of writers widely sundered by time and space; urges us to judge the doctrines by the positive evidence of those who have investigated them, not the negative testimony of those who have not; and insists on the absolute necessity of pureness of life in an Alchymist, as well as an inherent capacity to understand symbolism. He warmly advocates secrecy and allegorical teaching, as shown by the quaint quotations he makes from other authors, of which the following is a specimen: —

"Nor let any expect," saith he, "Comfortable Doctrine in our Books, who know not the true Keys, by which our Matter is brought forth from Darkness into the Light: For verily though we write for the Enlightening a true Son of Art, yet also for the fatal Blinding of all such Owls and Bats, who cannot behold the Light of the Sun, nor can endure the Splendour of our Moon. To such we propound rare Tricks, suiting to their sordid Fancy: To the Covetous, an easy way without Expense: To the Hasty, Rash and Unstable, multiplicity of Distillations."

The writer is very discursive, passing topic to topic and quoting numerous authors; but, though difficult to summarize, it is plain that his constant theme is the necessity for taking the Alchymical symbology in its highest sense. For instance, speaking of the Gold and Silver, he says: —

"And as the Author of the *Way to Bliss* has not only told us (among many others) where the *Seed of Gold* lies, *viz.*, in Gold; but how it lies, *viz.*, 'This Seed of Gold is his whole Body loosened and softened in his own Water; there is all your Stuff and Preparation.' So he hath also, with the same Candor, showed us the *Water* in which it *dies*, and with which it is *raised*."

About the Fire we read as follows: —

"This Fire has lain hid from many, a long time after they knew the Field in general, where the Seed was to be sown. The *fiery Furnace of Philosophers*, says one of them, 'lay hid from me long; but after I knew this, and how it was fitted to its proper Vessel, after a few days I beheld the admirable Brightness of our Water, which being seen, I could not but be amazed.' "

"S.S.D." has a most instructive "Introduction to Alchemy," preceding the text, in which the power of the will and the imagination is dealt with.

—H[enry] T. E[dge].

Notes:
1. "Review - A Short Enquiry concerning the Hermetic Art," edited by Wynn Westcott " by H[enry] T. E[dge] is reprinted from *Lucifer: A Theosophical Magazine*, Vol. 14; No. 11, London, July, 1894, p. 429.—D.K.
2. By "A Lover of Philalethes," edited by Dr. W. Wynn Westcott. London: Theosophical Publishing Society, 1894. Price 2*s*. 6*d*.—H.T.E.

BIBLIOGRAPHY

A Short Enquiry Concerning the Hermetick Art. Addressed to the Studious therein. By a Lover of Philalethes. To which is Annexed, A Collection from *Kabbala Denudata*, and Translation of the Chymical-Cabbalistical Treatise, Intituled, *Æsch-Mezareph*; or, *Purifying Fire*. London: Printed in the Year, 1714.

> [iv], 92, 83, [i], 71, [i] pp.: ill. [12mo.]
> ii p. Title page.
> iii-iv pp. The Publisher to the Reader.
> 92 pp. *The Hermetic Art* (Part I) in English.
> 83 pp. *Æsch-Mezareph* in English.
> 71 pp. *Æsch-Mezareph* in Latin and Hebrew.

The Short Enquiry Concerning the Hermetick Art (Which was printed with the Latin and English, *Æsch-Mezareph*) By a Lover of Philaletha. [Parts II & III.] London: Printed in the Year, 1715.

> [ii] x, 48, [ii], 59 pp.; [12mo.]
> [ii] p. Title page.
> i-x pp. Preface (to Parts II & III).
> 48 pp. *The Hermetic Art* (Part II) in English.
> 59 pp. *The Hermetic Art* (Part III) in English.

A Short Enquiry Concerning the Hermetic Art by A Lover of Philalethes. London 1714. *Collectanea Hermetica* Vol III. Preface by Non Omnis Moriar. An Introduction to Alchemy and Notes by S.S.D.D. London: Theosophical Publishing Society, 1894.

The Primary Books for Quotations

Elias Ashmole. *Theatrum Chemicum Britannicum*. Printed for *J[ohn] Grismond* for *Nath. Brooke* at the *Angel* in *Corn-hill*, 1652.

_____. *The Way of Bliss*. In Three Books. Printed for *John Grismond* for *Nath. Brook[e]* at the *Angel* in *Corn-hill*, 1658.

Roger Bacon. *The Mirror of Alchimy*. London, 1597.

Jean d'Espagnet. *The Hermetic Arcanum or, Secret*. Paris, 1623.

Geber (*Abu Musa Jafar al Sofi*). *The Works of Geber*. Faithfully Englished by Richard Russel. London: Printed for N.E. by Thomas James, and are to be sold by Robert Clavel, 1678.

Guglielmo Gratarolo. *Turba Philosophorum*. Basel, 1613.

Michael Maier. *Atalanta Fugiens: An Edition of the Emblems*. Latin edition. Oppenheim publisher, Johann Theodor de Bry, 1618.

Thomas Norton. "The Ordinall of Alchymie" in *Theatrum Chemicum Britannicum*. Edited by Elias Ashmole, 1652.

Eirenæus Philalethes. *Three Tracts of the Great Medicine of Philosophers for humane and metalline bodies*. Translated into English by a lover of art and them. London, 1694.–D.K.

_____. *Ripley Revived*. London: Printed for William Cooper at the Pellican on Little Britain, 1677.

_____. [*Secrets Reveal'd: or,*] *An Open Entrance to the Closed Palace of the King*. English translation. London, 1669. It was published in Latin as *Introitus Apertus ad Occlusum Regis Palatium* in Amsterdam, 1668.

Eugenius Philalethes. *Euphrates or the Waters of the East*. 1655.

George Ripley. "Compound of Alchemy" in *Theatrum Chemicum Britannicum*. London, 1652. (Also known as *The Twelve Gates*.)

Merian Matthaeus. *Musaeum Hermeticum* (*Hermetic Museum*). Expanded Latin edition. Frankfort, 1678.

Michael Sendivogius. *A New Light of Alchymie* (*Novum Lumen Chymicum*). Translated out of the Latin into English by J[ohn] F[rench]. London: Printed by Richard Cotes, for Thomas Williams, 1650.

NOTES

"CONTRIBUTORS."

———

DARCY KÜNTZ is the director of the Golden Dawn Research Trust which was founded in 1998. The Research Trust is preserving the teachings, ritual, history, practices, documents, letters, and books of the Hermetic Order of the Golden Dawn (as it existed between the dates 1887-1930). We are preserving this material so that the information may be available and remain accessible to scholars now and in the future. Some of his published works includes: *Complete Golden Dawn Cipher Manuscript* (1996); *Golden Dawn Sourcebook* (1996); *The Historic Structure of the Original Golden Dawn Temples* (1999); *The Golden Dawn American Source Book* (2000); *Sent From the Second Order* (2005); *Ancient Texts of the Golden Rosicrucians* (2008).

Florence Farr was a brilliant actress who joined the Order of the Golden Dawn in July 1890. She chose the motto "Sapientia Sapienti Dono Data", which translates as "Wisdom is a Gift given to the Wise". She was very active in the Order and even took on a number of administration roles. On 1 April 1897 she was appointment the Chief Adept in Anglia. As Chief Adept she dealt with a number of schisms which ultimately caused her to resigned from the Order in 1902. After leaving the Order she continued writing and published a number of books. She moved to Jaffna, Ceylon and become the principal of the Ramanathan Hindu Girls' College on 5 September 1912. There she died of breast Cancer on 29 April 1917.

Some of her published works include: *The Dancing Faun*, (1894); *Egyptian Magic.* (Collectanea Hermetica Vol. VIII), (1896); *Modern Woman: Her Intentions*, (1910); *The Music of Speech*, (1909); *The Mystery of Time. A Masque*, (1905); *The Solemnization of Jacklin: Some Adventures on the Search for Reality*, (1912); *The Way of Wisdom. An Investigation of the Meanings of the Letters of the Hebrew Alphabet, Considered as a Remnant of Chaldean Wisdom*, (1900); *The Magical Writings of Florence Farr*, (2012).

Tommy Westlund is a trained therapist in psychosynthesis, and since 1990 has pursued studies and research in esotericism and the Western Hermetic tradition. With an academic background in psychology, the history of religion, and the history of ideas, he writes and lectures internationally on esotericism, Alchemy, the Golden Dawn, Gnosticism, and Freemasonry. He is one of the founders of the initiatic Order of the Sodalitas Rosae+Crucis & Solis Alati, which perpetuates many of the old esoteric currents and Hermetic filiations of Europe, and also co-founded the Swedish Alchemical Academy in 2006, which offers alchemical courses, workshops, and literature.

WILLIAM WYNN WESTCOTT was one of the founders of the Order of the Golden Dawn. In the Order he used the motto V.H. Frater "Sapere Aude", which translates as "Dare to be wise". Westcott was involved in a number of Orders some of which are the Societas Rosicruciana In Anglia, Freemasonry, and the Coronati Lodge #2076, the premier Lodge of Masonic Research. Westcott wrote many medical and therapeutic works, but he is better known by his Masonic and Rosicrucian works, among them are: *The Sepher Yetzirah*; *The Isiac Tablet of Cardinal Bembo*; *An Essay on Alchemy*; *Numbers, Their Occult Power and Mystic Virtues*; *The Hieroglyphic Figures of Nicholas Flamel*, and numerous volumes of the *Collectanea Hermetica*.

www.ingramcontent.com/pod-product-compliance
Lightning Source LLC
Chambersburg PA
CBHW020359100426
42812CB00001B/119